PRAISE FOR

"Black writers have used writing and reading to create, find, and sometimes save their lives. Stephanie Stokes Oliver invites the reader into a black magic circle of incendiary, replenishing, and inspiring ideas, memories, and meditations on the power of literacy and imagination by the writers we treasure. It was a pleasure to re-read established classics and discover new classic arguments for the power of the written and read word."

—Marita Golden, author of
Living Out Loud: A Writer's Journey

"This electric and electrifying collection of voices serves to open a much-needed window onto the freedom struggle of black literature. It's a marvel and a genuine gift for readers everywhere."

—Wil Haygood, author of
The Butler: A Witness to History

"An enticing introduction to African-American writing from the 19th century to the present . . . This work of discovery, recovery, and uncovering is, for any reader, an eye-opener."

—Publishers Weekly

"An important and long overdue project . . . An essential collection for readers and students of black history and literature."

—Library Journal (starred review)

"An informative overview of African-American literature. Revelatory . . . moving . . . impressive."

—Kirkus Reviews

"Stephanie Stokes Oliver pulls together African American literary giants who seem to make literacy something that should be in bold neon letters. Indeed, the essays you'll find in here will make bookworms want to stand up and cheer."

—The Miami Times

"*Black Ink* presents the brilliant diversity of black thought in America while solidifying the importance of these writers within the greater context of the American literary tradition."

—Bustle

"[A]n inspiring anthology of excerpts from books and essays by 25 black icons on the dangers and joys of education."

—The Toronto Star

"A collection of great literary essays."

—Glory Edim, founder, Well-Read Black Girl

ALSO BY STEPHANIE STOKES OLIVER

Daily Cornbread
365 Secrets for a Healthy Mind, Body, and Spirit

Seven Soulful Secrets
For Finding Your Purpose and Minding Your Mission

Song for My Father
Memoir of an All-American Family

Frederick Douglass | Solomon Northup | Booker T. Washington | W. E. B. Du Bois | Zora Neale Hurston | Langston Hughes | James Baldwin | Malcolm X | Maya Angelou | Martin Luther King Jr. | Toni Morrison | Walter Dean Myers | Stokely Carmichael [Kwame Ture] | Alice Walker | Jamaica Kincaid | Henry Louis Gates Jr. | Terry McMillan | Junot Díaz | Edwidge Danticat | Colson Whitehead | Marlon James | Roxane Gay | Ta-Nehisi Coates | Chimamanda Ngozi Adichie | Bonus Feature: President Barack Obama

BLACK INK

LITERARY LEGENDS ON THE PERIL, POWER, AND PLEASURE OF READING AND WRITING

EDITED BY

STEPHANIE STOKES OLIVER

FOREWORD BY

NIKKI GIOVANNI

37INK

—

ATRIA

NEW YORK   LONDON   TORONTO   SYDNEY   NEW DELHI

37INK

ATRIA

An Imprint of Simon & Schuster, Inc.
1230 Avenue of the Americas
New York, NY 10020

First 37 INK/Atria Paperback edition December 2018

37INK / ATRIA PAPERBACK and colophon are trademarks of Simon & Schuster, Inc.

For information about special discounts for bulk purchases, please contact Simon & Schuster Special Sales at 1-866-506-1949 or business@simonandschuster.com.

The Simon & Schuster Speakers Bureau can bring authors to your live event. For more information, or to book an event, contact the Simon & Schuster Speakers Bureau at 1-866-248-3049 or visit our website at www.simonspeakers.com.

Interior design by Kyoko Watanabe

Manufactured in the United States of America

10 9 8 7 6 5 4 3 2

Library of Congress Cataloging-in-Publication Data is available.

ISBN 978-1-5011-5428-7
ISBN 978-1-5011-5429-4 (pbk)
ISBN 978-1-5011-5430-0 (ebook)

*For
the ancestors,
for you,
and for the
readers, writers, and thinkers
to come*

CONTENTS

ix

THE PLEASURE | 1968–2017

FOREWORD

Our First Stories

NIKKI GIOVANNI

Yolande Cornelia "Nikki" Giovanni grew up in Cincinnati, Ohio, and spent her summers with her grandparents in Knoxville, Tennessee, where she was born in 1943. Giovanni graduated with honors from her grandfather's alma mater, Fisk University. A world-renowned poet, author, commentator, activist, and educator, Giovanni has published volumes of poetry, nonfiction, essays, and children's books.

She gained initial fame in the 1960s, as a leading voice of the Black Arts Movement, in the time of the civil rights and Black Power struggles. Awarded seven NAACP Image Awards, she has been nominated for a Grammy and was a finalist for the National Book Award. Since 1987, she has served on the faculty of Virginia Tech, where she is a university distinguished professor.

Giovanni's literary greatness is on par with the twenty-five legendary writers included in this anthology. In the following foreword, she has graciously shared her own experiences in the tradition of the narrative of the book. She also sets the stage for what precedes the era of these writers in America—the horrific journey of the Middle Passage. While few of us ever think of it, overcoming language differences among the captured enslaved and then subsequently learning American English were among the first miracles along the path toward Black authorship as we know it today—from the peril of education to the power of literacy and then the pleasure of literature. First a moan, then a song, now a book.

t only makes sense to me that the first word those captured understood was "SOLD." They probably heard it so often, they thought that was their name. Off they were sent to various communities where they had to learn to talk to one another. The first language was a song.

They sang in the evening to comfort one another and in the morning to call us all to work. These folk built homes and communities. They had skills that were put to use to plant and harvest. Through the years, our ancestors found a way to understand we all are of the same community no matter where we came from. We helped one another. It is so easy to think we came from African communities with no knowledge of how to live together—which is just ridiculous.

No matter who we are or where we find ourselves, our first stories came in song. We have to remember Day Ten on the Slave Ship. On the first and second day we, the captured, were brought up to be washed with seawater and made to jump up and down to keep our muscles in some sort of shape. We could look to see the ending of the country, actually the continent, from which we'd come.

I once had a professor who had been so very kind to me. She had helped me be accepted in the Pennsylvania School of Social Work. When that was not working for me, she got me accepted in the new MFA program at Columbia University in New York City. Years later, I was in London for a poetry reading when her daughter called to say Louise had died. If ever there was a funeral at which I wanted to be present, it was hers. But the only way to get back to Philadelphia on time was on the Super Sonic Transport (SST) aircraft, also known as the Concorde. I was a young poet, and not having much money, I tried to see how that was possible. Then I realized: It didn't matter whether I could afford the flight. I just needed to get someone to give me a credit card so that I could charge my flight. Someone did. And I did.

The SST took off, and it went up and up—and up and up again.

They no longer have it, but it was actually a rocket, and there was only one seat on each side. I looked out my window as we continued to climb. The pilot finally said, "Ladies and Gentlemen, we are at sixty thousand feet . . . sixty-five thousand feet . . . seventy thousand feet." We could see the curve of the earth. It was totally fascinating.

My African ancestors probably did not enjoy seeing the push away, but on the fifth and sixth day to the New World they could look out or over, neither they nor I know which one, and see the ending of all they knew. We know that by the tenth day, all the white people on the ship were armed because those captured would now be fighting, if not for their lives, for their knowledge. We lost. Some of us were hanged. Some were thrown overboard. Some jumped. But those who understood that we were lost understood also that we had to rethink who we were or are.

I always like to think it was an older woman who was put back down in the hole who understood the loss. She knew she needed to say something to her people, though there is no such language as "African." So she reached into her soul and began a moan. And that moan was picked up and carried forth. By the time the ship reached what would be called America, those on that ship had one thing in common: a song.

We also found a God that we learned to worship and lean on. We took that same song from the slave ship to worship that God. And that song is what we are looking at now.

The black people who sold us and the white people who bought us never understood we were going to become a new people. We were going to build a new world. We were going to change the culinary habits of this world. How this world worshiped. How in this world we taught our children to be strong and go forward.

The enslavers thought if we were not allowed to read and write, we would not appreciate who we were becoming, but they were wrong. We wrote sometimes with paper and we always wrote with song. All of us passed our stories down on paper or through song. We fought for education, but we also in the cool of the evening passed down our stories around the fireplace.

My grandparents sat on the front porch at the end of day, after Grandmother had cooked our evening meal and I had washed the dishes, and talked with our neighbors. Some call it gossip; some call it history. We talked with one another. I learned on that porch to never argue with anyone who was stupid. To never try to persuade anyone who would never agree to help. I also learned to appreciate and love the folk who came to share a secret. To say when there would be a meeting. To share what was needed to get someone up North to school or safety. I learned to listen, to be patient, and most especially, I learned to cheerfully give: time, knowledge, money. What sadness it brings that we no longer sit on front porches and call to one another. What terrible sadness it is that we want the folk who sold us and the folk who purchased us to like us. We have to like ourselves. We have to love one another.

We write because we have evolved to another century. We write to be sure the words to the songs, and for those who understand, the notes to the music, get written down. We write because we are lonely and scared and we need to keep our hearts open. Black Ink, or as my student Jordan Holmes writes, Black Mail, comes to all of us because that's who we are and what we do it with. By definition, Black Mail is what we receive. And I am so glad that I do.

I like those folks on the ship who created that moan that became the spirituals that turned into jazz and blues and everything all the way up to rap and whatever will come next. We who do words are doing what we do. We are not trying to get folk who are frightened of us to be calm around us. We are reminding folk who love us that this is a good thing. Black Ink should be a soup or a drink or something we can embrace with pride. Black Lives Matter. *Black Ink* reminds us of why.

INTRODUCTION

Reading Matters

STEPHANIE STOKES OLIVER

Collectively, the pieces here serve as a testament to
the will, the struggle, and the difference that learning
to read, and then taking pen to paper, and now fingers
to computer, has made in American history.

t's **hard to** believe that the relaxing, recreational endeavor of reading a good book that so many of us savor and take for granted was, for more than two hundred years, not only illegal for most African Americans enslaved in many states of the South, but also punishable by death.

When it comes to voting rights, Black parents often admonish their grown children to be sure to exercise their freedom in every election, because people died in the fight to obtain the right to vote. The proof is not disputed. Black-and-white newsreels of African Americans being terrorized by state troopers, police dogs, and firehoses during protest marches against disenfranchisement in the 1960s have been continuously and dramatically included in documentaries and other films and news programs. They tell the story that riveted the nation's consciousness and caused American presidents to act.

The story of the struggle for full literacy among African Americans has yet to be documented as thoroughly. The purpose of *Black Ink: Literary Legends on the Peril, Power, and Pleasure of Reading and Writing* is to help fill that void.

Much like the griot of African oral history—the revered storyteller of the tribal history, what we would call now the keeper of "institutional memory"—we honor this struggle for literacy by passing on the words and wisdom of the writers included here. We have collected twenty-five of the most elite, brilliant, and wise Black writers of the African diaspora, voices that tell the story of the plight to read, write, and publish throughout generations of our nations. Of course, there are many, many more Black writers, authors, essayists, journalists, and academics that could have been included to make a multivolume comprehensive work. However, we endeavored to provide a satisfying sampler of pieces that may motivate the reader to dig deeper and check out the original books from which these works were excerpted, as well as to explore additional Black authors and essays not included.

Individually, the authors of *Black Ink* possess what Dr. Greg Carr, chair of the Afro-American Studies program at Howard University, calls the "deep critical literacy and content mastery necessary to meet intellectual curiosity, spur academic growth, satisfy the need to know, and to act to transform one's self and the world." Collectively, the pieces here serve as a testament to the will, the struggle, and the difference that learning to read and then taking pen to paper, and now fingers to computer, has made in American history.

As poet Nikki Giovanni, one of America's foremost literary legends, so brilliantly reminds us in her foreword, the first word in that foreign language, English, understood by the captive ancestors on these shores just may well have been "SOLD." In my favorite of Nikki's poems, "My House," she evokes the African American loss of our mother tongue in the transport across the Middle Passage and in our oppressive New World from which I feel we have never fully recovered:

> *english isn't a good language*
> *to express emotion through*
> *mostly i imagine because people*
> *try to speak english instead*
> *of trying to speak through it . . .*

Starting in the early 1800s, over approximately twenty-five decades up to today, the twenty-five writers of these expository essays of *Black Ink* explain to us the struggle and the joys of overcoming the challenges of reading and writing. They are: Frederick Douglass, Solomon Northup, Booker T. Washington, W. E. B. Du Bois, Zora Neale Hurston, Langston Hughes, James Baldwin, Malcolm X, Maya Angelou, Martin Luther King Jr., Toni Morrison, Walter Dean Myers, Stokely Carmichael [Kwame Ture], Alice Walker, Jamaica Kincaid, Henry Louis Gates Jr., Terry McMillan, Junot Díaz, Edwidge Danticat, Colson Whitehead, Marlon James, Roxane Gay, Ta-Nehisi Coates, Chimamanda Ngozi Adichie, and President Barack Obama, in an exclusive interview with *New York Times* book critic Michiko Kakutani. These pieces reflect the phenomenal African American progress from when it was illegal to learn to read—and

Frederick Douglass resisted, escaped, and claimed his freedom—up
to the election of our first Black President of the United States, an
avid reader and mega-bestselling author.

The voices are classic and contemporary, historic and avant-garde.
Some reflect the unique perspective, sensibility, and wisdom of the
immigrant. Many of the writers were born in the African and Caribbean diaspora and relocated to the United States, such as Stokely
Carmichael (Trinidad), Jamaica Kincaid (Antigua), Junot Díaz
(Dominican Republic), Edwidge Danticat (Haiti), Marlon James
(Jamaica), and Chimamanda Ngozi Adichie (Nigeria). Others were
born in the States and eventually found a place that felt more like
home elsewhere and died there, including W. E. B. Du Bois (Ghana)
and James Baldwin (France). Stokely Carmichael, who grew up in
New York City, made his transition in Guinea, in West Africa.

Within the larger American literary tradition, Black voices are
often marginalized or included as tokenism. Here, they are front
and center, loud and clear, humble and proud, humorous and dead
serious. Like ink itself, *Black Ink* is what gives us common ground
whether in the ink made with tree bark by Solomon Northup (author
of *Twelve Years a Slave*) to write a letter that would secure his freedom
in 1853 or in the digital ink of our e-readers that now allow us to
download novels, such as Colson Whitehead's highly acclaimed *The
Underground Railroad*, awarded the National Book Award (2016) and
the Pulitzer Prize (2017), and chosen in 2016 by Oprah's Book Club.
Oprah Winfrey's book discussion group, launched in 1996 during
the successful twenty-five-year run of her internationally viewed
television program, and her influence on the world of publishing, is
another phenomenon of Black literary achievement. "In the black" is
a positive financial term of success, to which we all aspire.

As the editor of *Essence* and, later, editor in chief of *Heart & Soul*
magazine, I had the special honor of assigning and editing feature
pieces by great authors. My interest in reading literature was passion-
ately developed while taking an African American lit course at Howard University. I graduated the year that Toni Morrison edited the
groundbreaking historical collection *The Black Book* (an inspiration

for this anthology). After college, working as a junior editor at one of the top women's general interest magazines, *Glamour*, I was swept into an exciting time of emerging female voices in publishing: Nora Ephron was humoring us with her collection of essays, *Crazy Salad*; Toni Morrison was publishing her third novel, *Song of Solomon*; Alice Walker published an essay in *Ms.* magazine about rediscovering the work of Zora Neale Hurston. At *Essence*, I worked with a brilliant team of predominantly Black women editors who reveled in their duty to present to the African American reading public the best and brightest African American writers. *Essence* succeeded in providing a home for our literary writers who may not have been applauded at all or as often by the White-run literary magazines of the day. Many of the writers first published in *Essence* were then able to secure major book publishing deals. And those who were recognized by the publishing world relied on us to spread the word of their new releases.

In those premillennial times, before celebrities dominated magazine covers and the center-well features of publications, it was writers, readers, and thinkers who were revered. There wasn't one celebrity in whose company I would have preferred to be over author and poet Maya Angelou. When her memoir *The Heart of the Woman* was published in the mid-1980s, I had the plum assignment to interview her in her North Carolina kitchen as she made spaghetti. I learned that for Angelou, poetry was not just a professional pursuit but also a personal passion. When my daughter was born, she sent the gift of her favorite poems to share with my child—not bound volumes, but a thoughtfully chosen "anthology" of photocopied pages from books and magazines that have been saved and cherished as much or more than any of her published books. On the handwritten note attached Angelou wrote to Anique, "I pray you grow strong, well, and beautiful . . . and with this poetry of joy!"

There was no greater delight conducting a photo shoot than at the Cincinnati home of Nikki Giovanni, and noticing her wall-to-wall bookshelves had been personally organized according to the Dewey decimal system. When Alice Walker became the first Black woman to win a Pulitzer Prize for Fiction, and also to grace the cover of *Essence* in dreadlocks—on a September fashion issue, no less—it was a great moment for the magazine. James Baldwin was still highly regarded in 1987, and showed his love for the magazine, writing an original piece for *Essence* at the time of his untimely passing that remains unpublished to this day. In 1992, when Terry McMillan drew crowds of Black women readers that formed lines around the block of bookstores at which she read from *Waiting to Exhale*, she made publishing history. The next year, when Toni Morrison became the first African American woman to win the Nobel Prize in Literature, it was a triumph for the world of letters and the literary aspirations and achievements of a people. I recall a lovely party thrown in her honor at the Gracie Mansion home of the first Black mayor of New York City, David Dinkins, Morrison's Howard University classmate.

Black Ink endeavors to replicate the feeling of being in the room with them and others. Many of the authors are novelists. Their award-winning and bestselling books are works of fiction from the brilliant imaginations and shared memories of genius minds. In curating the anthology, I attempted to discover their interior worlds. What personal, real-life experiences informed their work? As a journalist, I wanted to know what drove the early authors to learn to read, then what motivated the later ones to break down barriers to be published. I wondered what made it possible to overcome the seemingly impossible racism to evolve from what Langston Hughes biographer Arnold Rampersad describes as the "literature of necessity to the inclusion of leisure."

Zora Neale Hurston wrote novels, but in her autobiography, *Dust Tracks on a Road*, excerpted here, she lamented that "Negroes were supposed to write about the Race Problem." Novelist Chimamanda Ngozi Adichie warned almost seventy years later in a TED Talk speech that gained international attention, about the danger of the benign neglect of diversity and the feigned privilege of the literary lie of the "single story." The strength of *Black Ink* is in the common knowledge among the writers of the power of inserting our diverse experiences into the "mainstream" and the courage to make change with words.

This collection of essays has been carefully curated from memoirs, book introductions, newspaper articles, speeches, and media interviews. Some of the selections from book-length works were meticulously condensed. Reprint permissions were painstakingly obtained from the authors, agents, and publishers. *Black Ink* is presented in three parts: "The Peril," "The Power," and "The Pleasure." The order of the pieces is chronological from the birth of each writer, with the exception of Frederick Douglass, who was born after Solomon Northup, but because his memoir was published first, and exposes the danger of "reading while Black" when it was illegal, we have put his story as the lead. The last section, "Pleasure," is called that because this generation does enjoy a degree of being able to read and write what they please, as Roxane Gay's delightful story expresses, and Colson Whitehead's humorous take on "How to Write" offers. However, the seriousness of the essays of Junot Díaz, Edwidge Danticat, and Marlon James could also fall under the heading of "Purpose."

Life has progressed for the better for African Americans since the founding of the United States of America. These two dozen of our top, most elite writers across that time share from the heart their personal stories of inspiration and motivation in literacy and literature. Their cumulative freedom of expression, literary achievements, Nobel Prizes, Pulitzer Prizes, National Book Awards, NAACP Image Awards, and even Presidential Summer Reading Lists exemplify what poet Maya Angelou describes in her poem "Still I Rise" as "the hope and the dream of the slave."

The presidency of Barack Hussein Obama gave us a glimpse of the manifestation of that hope and dream. In 2008, the United States elected not only the first African American president, but also a most prolific author in chief. Like *Narrative of the Life of Frederick Douglass*, published in 1845, *Dreams from My Father* is President Obama's excellent coming-of-age memoir. Released exactly 150 years later when Obama was just thirty-four years old and embarking on his political life, *Dreams* goes into great detail about the importance of books in developing his Black identity. *New York*

Times book critic Michiko Kakutani described *Dreams from My Father* as surely the most "evocative, lyrical, and candid autobiography written by a future president." Her 2009 essay "From Books, New President Found Voice" went on to state it "suggests that throughout his life he has turned to books as a way of acquiring insights and information from others—as a means of breaking out of the bubble of self-hood and, more recently, the bubble of power and fame. He recalls that he read James Baldwin, Ralph Ellison, Langston Hughes, Richard Wright, and W. E. B. Du Bois when he was an adolescent in an effort to come to terms with his racial identity . . ." Of all the books Obama read that helped shape him, he wrote in his memoir, "Only Malcolm X's autobiography seemed to offer something different. His repeated acts of self-creation spoke to me; the blunt poetry of his words, his unadorned insistence on respect, promised a new and uncompromising order, martial in its discipline, forged through sheer force of will."

Years later, near the end of his second term in office, the president spoke of how his love of literacy and his international upbringing allowed him to find common ground with world leaders. In 2016, at the funeral of former Israeli president and prime minister Shimon Peres, President Obama said that he and Peres "shared a love of words and books and history. And, perhaps like most politicians, we shared too great a joy in hearing ourselves talk. . . . But beyond that, I think our friendship was rooted in the fact that I could somehow see myself in his story and maybe he could see himself in mine."

That, I feel, is a most important part literature plays in our lives. In print books, we can study and cultivate greatness. We can learn about one another in the safety of our own homes and the privacy of our electronic devices, without concern over saying the wrong thing or being politically incorrect. With audiobooks, we can listen in on great storytelling, sans the current intrusion of the arguing and rancor of media talking heads. Reading gives us knowledge and wisdom that can bring us together to make change for the better in our lives, our communities, our countries, and our world.

Reading matters. Writing matters. Enjoy.

THE PERIL

1800–1900

There was a time in our country when it was illegal
for enslaved people to learn to read and write,
yet the power of the human spirit prevailed.

Suspected of Having a Book

FREDERICK DOUGLASS

It was unlawful, as well as unsafe,
to teach a slave to read.

Frederick Augustus Washington Bailey Douglass (1818–1895), the most prominent leader in the antislavery abolitionist movement, was also a women's rights advocate, a US diplomat, and a bestselling author of two autobiographies.

In this passage from *Narrative of the Life of Frederick Douglass, an American Slave, Written by Himself*, originally published in 1845 and excerpted here from the 2010 edition featuring an introductory essay by Angela Y. Davis, Douglass tells the powerful story of his enslaved childhood and his awakening to disobey his White slave masters by secretly teaching himself to read, resist, escape, and ultimately achieve his freedom.

My new mistress proved to be all she appeared when I first met her at the door—a woman of the kindest heart and finest feelings. She had never had a slave under her control previously to myself, and prior to her marriage she had been dependent upon her own industry for a living. She was by trade a weaver; and by constant application to her business she had been in a good degree preserved from the blighting and dehumanizing effects of slavery. I was utterly astonished at her goodness. I scarcely knew how to behave towards her. She was entirely unlike any other white woman I had ever seen. I could not approach her as I was accustomed to approach other white ladies. My early instruction was all out of place. The crouching servility, usually so acceptable a quality in a slave, did not answer when manifested toward her. Her favor was not gained by it; she seemed to be disturbed by it. She did not deem it impudent or unmannerly for a slave to look her in the face. The meanest slave was put fully at ease in her presence, and none left without feeling better for having seen her. Her face was made of heavenly smiles, and her voice of tranquil music.

But alas! this kind heart had but a short time to remain such. The fatal poison of irresponsible power was already in her hands, and soon commenced its infernal work. That cheerful eye, under the influence of slavery, soon became red with rage; that voice, made all of sweet accord, changed to one of harsh and horrid discord; and that angelic face gave place to that of a demon.

Very soon after I went to live with Mr. and Mrs. Auld, she very kindly commenced to teach me the A, B, C. After I had learned this, she assisted me in learning to spell words of three or four letters. Just at this point of my progress, Mr. Auld found out what was going on, and at once forbade Mrs. Auld to instruct me further, telling her, among other things, that it was unlawful, as well as unsafe, to teach a slave to read. To use his own words, further, he said, "If you give a nigger an inch, he will take an ell. A nigger should know nothing but to obey his master—to do as he is told to do. Learning would spoil

4

the best nigger in the world. Now," said he, "if you teach that nigger (speaking of myself) how to read, there would be no keeping him. It would forever unfit him to be a slave. He would at once become unmanageable, and of no value to his master. As to himself, it could do him no good, but a great deal of harm. It would make him discontented and unhappy." These words sank deep into my heart, stirred up sentiments within that lay slumbering, and called into existence an entirely new train of thought. It was a new and special revelation, explaining dark and mysterious things, with which my youthful understanding had struggled, but struggled in vain. I now understood what had been to me a most perplexing difficulty—to wit, the white man's power to enslave the black man. It was a grand achievement, and I prized it highly. From that moment, I understood the pathway from slavery to freedom. It was just what I wanted, and I got it at a time when I the least expected it. Whilst I was saddened by the thought of losing the aid of my kind mistress, I was gladdened by the invaluable instruction which, by the merest accident, I had gained from my master. Though conscious of the difficulty of learning without a teacher, I set out with high hope, and a fixed purpose, at whatever cost of trouble, to learn how to read. The very decided manner with which he spoke, and strove to impress his wife with the evil consequences of giving me instruction, served to convince me that he was deeply sensible of the truths he was uttering. It gave me the best assurance that I might rely with the utmost confidence on the results which, he said, would flow from teaching me to read. What he most dreaded, that I most desired. What he most loved, that I most hated. That which to him was a great evil, to be carefully shunned, was to me a great good, to be diligently sought; and the argument which he so warmly urged, against my learning to read, only served to inspire me with a desire and determination to learn. In learning to read, I owe almost as much to the bitter opposition of my master, as to the kindly aid of my mistress. I acknowledge the benefit of both.

I had resided but a short time in Baltimore before I observed a marked difference, in the treatment of slaves, from that which I had witnessed in the country. A city slave is almost a freeman, compared with a slave on the plantation. He is much better fed and clothed, and enjoys privileges altogether unknown to the slave on the plantation. There is a vestige of decency, a sense of shame, that does much to curb and check those outbreaks of atrocious cruelty so commonly enacted upon the plantation. He is a desperate slaveholder, who will shock the humanity of his non-slaveholding neighbors with the cries of his lacerated slave. Few are willing to incur the odium attaching to the reputation of being a cruel master; and above all things, they would not be known as not giving a slave enough to eat. Every city slaveholder is anxious to have it known of him, that he feeds his slaves well; and it is due to them to say, that most of them do give their slaves enough to eat. There are, however, some painful exceptions to this rule. Directly opposite to us, on Philpot Street, lived Mr. Thomas Hamilton. He owned two slaves. Their names were Henrietta and Mary. Henrietta was about twenty-two years of age, Mary was about fourteen; and of all the mangled and emaciated creatures I ever looked upon, these two were the most so. His heart must be harder than stone, that could look upon these unmoved. The head, neck, and shoulders of Mary were literally cut to pieces. I have frequently felt her head, and found it nearly covered with festering sores, caused by the lash of her cruel mistress. I do not know that her master ever whipped her, but I have been an eye-witness to the cruelty of Mrs. Hamilton. I used to be in Mr. Hamilton's house nearly every day. Mrs. Hamilton used to sit in a large chair in the middle of the room, with a heavy cowskin always by her side, and scarce an hour passed during the day but was marked by the blood of one of these slaves. The girls seldom passed her without her saying, "Move faster, you *black gip!*" at the same time giving them a blow with the cowskin over the head or shoulders, often drawing the blood. She would then say, "Take that, you *black gip!*"—continuing, "If you don't move faster, I'll move you!" Added to the cruel lashings to which these slaves were subjected, they were kept nearly half-starved. They seldom knew what it was to eat a full meal. I have seen Mary contending with the pigs for the offal thrown into the street.

So much was Mary kicked and cut to pieces, that she was oftener called *"pecked"* than by her name.

———

I lived in Master Hugh's family about seven years. During this time, I succeeded in learning to read and write. In accomplishing this, I was compelled to resort to various stratagems. I had no regular teacher. My mistress, who had kindly commenced to instruct me, had, in compliance with the advice and direction of her husband, not only ceased to instruct, but had set her face against my being instructed by any one else. It is due, however, to my mistress to say of her, that she did not adopt this course of treatment immediately. She at first lacked the depravity indispensable to shutting me up in mental darkness. It was at least necessary for her to have some training in the exercise of irresponsible power, to make her equal to the task of treating me as though I were a brute.

My mistress was, as I have said, a kind and tender-hearted woman; and in the simplicity of her soul she commenced, when I first went to live with her, to treat me as she supposed one human being ought to treat another. In entering upon the duties of a slaveholder, she did not seem to perceive that I sustained to her the relation of a mere chattel, and that for her to treat me as a human being was not only wrong, but dangerously so. Slavery proved as injurious to her as it did to me. When I went there, she was a pious, warm, and tender-hearted woman. There was no sorrow or suffering for which she had not a tear. She had bread for the hungry, clothes for the naked, and comfort for every mourner that came within her reach. Slavery soon proved its ability to divest her of these heavenly qualities. Under its influence, the tender heart became stone, and the lamblike disposition gave way to one of tiger-like fierceness. The first step in her downward course was in her ceasing to instruct me. She now commenced to practise her husband's precepts. She finally became even more violent in her opposition than her husband himself. She was not satisfied with simply doing as well as he had commanded; she seemed anxious to do better. Nothing seemed to make her more angry than to see me with a newspaper. She seemed to think that here lay the danger. I have had her rush at me with a face made all up of fury, and snatch from me a newspaper, in a manner that fully revealed her apprehension. She was an apt woman; and a little experience soon demonstrated, to her satisfaction, that education and slavery were incompatible with each other.

From this time I was most narrowly watched. If I was in a separate room any considerable length of time, I was sure to be suspected of having a book, and was at once called to give an account of myself. All this, however, was too late. The first step had been taken. Mistress, in teaching me the alphabet, had given me the *inch*, and no precaution could prevent me from taking the *ell*.

The plan which I adopted, and the one by which I was most successful, was that of making friends of all the little white boys whom I met in the street. As many of these as I could, I converted into teachers. With their kindly aid, obtained at different times and in different places, I finally succeeded in learning to read. When I was sent of errands, I always took my book with me, and by going one part of my errand quickly, I found time to get a lesson before my return. I used also to carry bread with me, enough of which was always in the house, and to which I was always welcome; for I was much better off in this regard than many of the poor white children in our neighborhood. This bread I used to bestow upon the hungry little urchins, who, in return, would give me that more valuable bread of knowledge. I am strongly tempted to give the names of two or three of those little boys, as a testimonial of the gratitude and affection I bear them; but prudence forbids;—not that it would injure me, but it might embarrass them; for it is almost an unpardonable offence to teach slaves to read in this Christian country. It is enough to say of the dear little fellows, that they lived on Philpot Street, very near Durgin and Bailey's shipyard. I used to talk this matter of slavery over with them. I would sometimes say to them, I wished I could be as free as they would be when they got to be men. "You will be free as soon as you are twenty-one, *but I am a slave for life*! Have not I as good a right to be free as you have?" These words used to trouble them; they would express for me the liveliest sympathy, and console me with the hope that something would occur by which I might be free.

I was now about twelve years old, and the thought of being *a slave for life* began to bear heavily upon my heart. Just about this time, I got hold of a book entitled "The Columbian Orator." Every opportunity I got, I used to read this book. Among much of other interesting matter, I found in it a dialogue between a master and his slave. The slave was represented as having run away from his master three times. The dialogue represented the conversation which took place between them, when the slave was retaken the third time. In the dialogue, the whole argument in behalf of slavery was brought forward by the master, all of which was disposed of by the slave. The slave was made to say some very smart as well as impressive things in reply to his master—things which had the desired though unexpected effect; for the conversation resulted in the voluntary emancipation of the slave on the part of the master.

In the same book, I met with one of Sheridan's mighty speeches on and in behalf of Catholic emancipation. These were choice documents to me. I read them over and over again with unabated interest. They gave tongue to interesting thoughts of my own soul, which had frequently flashed through my mind, and died away for want of utterance. The moral which I gained from the dialogue was the power of truth over the conscience of even a slaveholder. What I got from Sheridan was a bold denunciation of slavery, and a powerful vindication of human rights. The reading of these documents enabled me to utter my thoughts, and to meet the arguments brought forward to sustain slavery; but while they relieved me of one difficulty, they brought on another even more painful than the one of which I was relieved. The more I read, the more I was led to abhor and detest my enslavers. I could regard them in no other light than a bank of successful robbers, who had left their homes, and gone to Africa, and stolen us from our homes, and in a strange land reduced us to slavery. I loathed them as being the meanest as well as the most wicked of men. As I read and contemplated the subject, behold! that very discontentment which Master Hugh had predicted would follow my learning to read had already come, to torment and sting my soul to unutterable anguish. As I writhed under it, I would at times feel that learning to read had been a curse rather than a blessing. It had given me a view of my wretched condition, without the remedy. It opened my eyes to the horrible pit, but to no ladder upon which to get out. In moments of agony, I envied my fellow-slaves for their stupidity. I have often wished myself a beast. I preferred the condition of the meanest reptile to my own. Any thing, no matter what, to get rid of thinking! It was this everlasting thinking of my condition that tormented me. There was no getting rid of it. It was pressed upon me by every object within sight or hearing, animate or inanimate. The silver trump of freedom had roused my soul to eternal wakefulness. Freedom now appeared, to disappear no more forever. It was heard in every sound, and seen in every thing. It was ever present to torment me with a sense of my wretched condition. I saw nothing without seeing it, I heard nothing without hearing it, and felt nothing without feeling it. It looked from every star, it smiled in every calm, breathed in every wind, and moved in every storm.

I often found myself regretting my own existence, and wishing myself dead; and but for the hope of being free, I have no doubt but that I should have killed myself, or done something for which I should have been killed. While in this state of mind, I was eager to hear any one speak of slavery. I was a ready listener. Every little while, I could hear something about the abolitionists. It was some time before I found what the word meant. It was always used in such connections as to make it an interesting word to me. If a slave ran away and succeeded in getting clear, or if a slave killed his master, set fire to a barn, or did any thing very wrong in the mind of a slaveholder, it was spoken of as the fruit of *abolition*. Hearing the word in this connection very often, I set about learning what it meant. The dictionary afforded me little or no help. I found it was "the act of abolishing;" but then I did not know what was to be abolished. Here I was perplexed. I did not dare to ask any one about its meaning, for I was satisfied that it was something they wanted me to know very little about. After a patient waiting, I got one of our city papers, containing an account of the number of petitions from the north, praying for the abolition of slavery in the District of Columbia, and of the slave trade between the States. From this time I understood the words *abolition* and *abolitionist*, and always drew near when that word was spoken, expecting to hear something of importance to myself and fellow-slaves. The light broke in upon me by degrees. I went one day down on the wharf of Mr. Waters; and seeing two Irishmen unloading a scow of stone, I went, unasked, and helped them. When we had finished, one of them came to me and asked me if I were a slave. I told him I was. He asked, "Are ye a slave for life?" I told him that I was. The good Irishman seemed to be deeply affected by the statement. He said to the other that it was a pity so fine a little fellow as myself should be a slave for life. He said it was a shame to hold me. They both advised me to run away to the north; that I should find friends there, and that I should be free. I pretended not to be interested in what they said, and treated them as if I did not understand them; for I feared they might be treacherous. White men have been known to encourage slaves to escape, and then, to get the reward, catch them and return them to their masters. I was afraid that these seemingly good men might use me so; but I nevertheless remembered their advice, and from that time I resolved to run away. I looked forward to a time at which it would be safe for me to escape. I was too young to think of doing so immediately; besides, I wished to learn how to write, as I might have occasion to write my own pass. I consoled myself with the hope that I should one day find a good chance. Meanwhile, I would learn to write.

The idea as to how I might learn to write was suggested to me by being in Durgin and Bailey's ship-yard, and frequently seeing the ship carpenters, after hewing, and getting a piece of timber ready for use, write on the timber the name of that part of the ship for which it was intended. When a piece of timber was intended for the larboard side, it would be marked thus—"L." When a piece was for the starboard side, it would be marked thus—"S." A piece for the larboard side forward, would be marked thus—"L. F." When a piece

was for starboard side forward, it would be marked thus—"S. F." For
larboard aft, it would be marked thus—"L. A." For starboard aft, it
would be marked thus—"S. A." I soon learned the names of these
letters, and for what they were intended when placed upon a piece of
timber in the ship-yard. I immediately commenced copying them,
and in a short time was able to make the four letters named. After
that, when I met with any boy who I knew could write, I would tell
him I could write as well as he. The next word would be, "I don't
believe you. Let me see you try it." I would then make the letters
which I had been so fortunate to learn, and ask him to beat that. In
this way I got a good many lessons in writing, which it is quite possible I should never have gotten in any other way. During this time,
my copy-book was the board fence, brick wall, and pavement; my
pen and ink was a lump of chalk. With these, I learned mainly how
to write. I then commenced and continued copying the Italics in
Webster's Spelling Book, until I could make them all without looking on the book. By this time, my little Master Thomas had gone
to school, and learned how to write, and had written over a number
of copy-books. These had been brought home, and shown to some
of our near neighbors, and then laid aside. My mistress used to go
to class meeting at the Wilk Street meeting house every Monday
afternoon, and leave me to take care of the house. When left thus, I
used to spend the time in writing in the spaces left in Master Thomas's copy-book, copying what he had written. I continued to do this
until I could write a hand very similar to that of Master Thomas.
Thus, after a long, tedious effort for years, I finally succeeded in
learning how to write.

Nine Years Deprived of
a Sheet of Paper

SOLOMON NORTHUP

I succeeded in making ink from bark,
manufactured a pen, and when all were
asleep in the cabin, by the light of the coals,
I managed to complete a lengthy epistle.

Born free in 1808, Solomon Northup was reared and educated in the town of Minerva in Essex County, New York. As a young adult, the husband and father of three was recognized as a talented violinist. In 1841, two men propositioned Northup to travel to Washington, DC, for a violin performance. He was told that he would be well paid for the short trip. Instead, Northup was assaulted and drugged, and kidnapped and sold as if he were a slave.

It took him until 1853 to secure his freedom, but his incredible memoir, *Twelve Years a Slave*, was soon published and enthusiastically received. He sued his kidnappers, but they were not convicted. The rest of his life seems to have proceeded peacefully in obscurity until his death, which, coincidentally, occurred around the time of the Emancipation.

In 2013, the story of his captivity—an abyss of oppression, abuse, and horror he had never known—was released as a feature film that gained international acclaim, including the Academy Award for Best Picture of the Year. Since 1999 in Saratoga, New York, there has been an annual Solomon Northup Day celebration on the third Saturday in July.

Here, in his own words vividly detailed in his 1853 memoir, *Twelve*

Years a Slave, Northup eloquently relays how he felt about, and coped with, his enslavement, not knowing when or if he would ever be rescued. Most compelling is his account of how literacy provided the hope and foundation of his constant attempts to escape by the simple, then deadly, means of writing a letter.

With the exception of my trip to St. Mary's parish, and my absence during the cane-cutting seasons, I was constantly employed on the plantation of Master Epps. He was considered but a small planter, not having a sufficient number of hands to require the services of an overseer, acting in the latter capacity himself. Not able to increase his force, it was his custom to hire during the hurry of cotton-picking.

On larger estates, employing fifty or a hundred, or perhaps two hundred hands, an overseer is deemed indispensable. These gentlemen ride into the field on horseback, without an exception, to my knowledge, armed with pistols, bowie knife, whip, and accompanied by several dogs. They follow, equipped in this fashion, in rear of the slaves, keeping a sharp lookout upon them all. The requisite qualifications in an overseer are utter heartlessness, brutality and cruelty. It is his business to produce large crops, and if that is accomplished, no matter what amount of suffering it may have cost. The presence of the dogs are necessary to overhaul a fugitive who may take to his heels, as is sometimes the case, when faint or sick, he is unable to maintain his row, and unable, also, to endure the whip. The pistols are reserved for any dangerous emergency, there having been instances when such weapons were necessary. Goaded into uncontrollable madness, even the slave will sometimes turn upon his oppressor. The gallows were standing at Marksville last January, upon which one was executed a year ago for killing his overseer. It occurred not many miles from Epps' plantation on Red River. The slave was given his task at splitting rails. In the course of the day the overseer sent him on an errand, which occupied so much time that it was not possible for him to perform the task. The next day he was called to an account, but the loss of time occasioned by the errand was no excuse, and he was ordered to kneel and bare his back for the reception of the lash. They were in the woods alone—beyond the reach of sight or hearing. The boy submitted until maddened at such injustice, and insane with pain, he sprang to his feet, and seizing an axe, literally chopped the overseer in pieces. He made no attempt whatever at concealment, but hastening to his master, related the whole affair, and declared himself ready to expiate the wrong by the sacrifice of his life. He was led to the scaffold, and while the rope was around his neck, maintained an undismayed and fearless bearing, and with his last words justified the act.

Besides the overseer, there are drivers under him the number being in proportion to the number of hands in the field. The drivers are black, who, in addition to the performance of their equal share of work, are compelled to do the whipping of their several gangs. Whips hang around their necks, and if they fail to use them thoroughly, are whipped themselves. They have a few privileges, however; for example, in cane-cutting the hands are not allowed to sit down long enough to eat their dinners. Carts filled with corn cake, cooked at the kitchen, are driven into the field at noon. The cake is distributed by the drivers, and must be eaten with the least possible delay.

When the slave ceases to perspire, as he often does when taxed beyond his strength, he falls to the ground and becomes entirely helpless. It is then the duty of the driver to drag him into the shade of the standing cotton or cane, or of a neighboring tree, where he dashes buckets of water upon him, and uses other means of bringing out perspiration again, when he is ordered to his place, and compelled to continue his labor.

At Huff Power, when I first came to Epps', Tom, one of Roberts' negroes, was driver. He was a burly fellow, and severe in the extreme. After Epps' removal to Bayou Boeuf, that distinguished honor was conferred upon myself. Up to the time of my departure I had to wear a whip about my neck in the field. If Epps was present, I dared not show any lenity, not having the Christian fortitude of a certain well-known Uncle Tom sufficiently to brave his wrath, by refusing to perform the office. In that way, only, I escaped the immediate martyrdom he suffered, and withal, saved my companions much suffering, as it proved in the end. Epps, I soon found, whether actually in the field or not, had his eyes pretty generally upon us. From the piazza, from behind some adjacent tree, or other concealed point of observation, he was perpetually on the watch. If one of us had been backward or idle through the day, we were apt to be told all about it on returning to the quarters, and as it was a matter of principle with him to reprove every offence of that kind that came within his knowledge, the offender not only was certain of receiving a castigation for his tardiness, but I likewise was punished for permitting it.

If, on the other hand, he had seen me use the lash freely, the man was satisfied. "Practice makes perfect," truly; and during my eight years' experience as a driver, I learned to handle the whip with marvelous dexterity and precision, throwing the last within a hair's breadth of the back, the ear, the nose, without, however, touching either of them. If Epps was observed at a distance, or we had reason to apprehend he was sneaking somewhere in the vicinity, I would commence plying the lash vigorously, when, according to arrangement, they would squirm and screech as if in agony, although not one of them had in fact been even grazed. Patsey would take occasion, if he made his appearance presently, to mumble in his hearing some complaints that Platt was lashing them the whole time, and Uncle Abram, with an appearance of honesty peculiar to himself, would declare roundly I had just whipped them worse than General Jackson whipped the enemy of New-Orleans. If Epps was not drunk, and in one of his beastly humors, this was, in general, satisfactory. If he was, some one or more of us must suffer, as a matter of course. Sometimes his violence assumed a dangerous form, placing the lives of his human stock in jeopardy. On one occasion the drunken madman thought to amuse himself by cutting my throat.

He had been absent at Holmesville, in attendance at a shooting match, and none of us were aware of his return. While hoeing by the side of Patsey, she exclaimed, in a low voice, suddenly, "Platt d'ye see old Hog-Jaw beckoning me to come to him?"

Glancing sideways, I discovered him in the edge of the field, motioning and grimacing, as was his habit when half-intoxicated. Aware of his lewd intentions, Patsey began to cry. I whispered her not to look up, and to continue at her work, as if she had not ob-

served him. Suspecting the truth of the matter, however, he soon
staggered up to me in a great rage.

"What did you say to Pats?" he demanded, with an oath. I made
him some evasive answer, which only had the effect of increasing his
violence.

"How long have you owned this plantation, *say*, you d——d
nigger?" he inquired, with a malicious sneer, at the same time taking hold of my shirt collar with one hand, and thrusting the other
into his pocket. "Now I'll cut your black throat; that's what I'll do,"
drawing his knife from his pocket as he said it. But with one hand
he was unable to open it, until finally seizing the blade in his teeth,
I saw he was about to succeed, and felt the necessity of escaping
from him, for in his present reckless state, it was evident he was not
joking, by any means. My shirt was open in front, and as I turned
round quickly and sprang from him, while he still retained his gripe,
it was stripped entirely from my back. There was no difficulty now
in eluding him. He would chase me until out of breath, then stop
until it was recovered, swear, and renew the chase again. Now he
would command me to come to him, now endeavor to coax me,
but I was careful to keep at a respectful distance. In this manner
we made the circuit of the field several times, he making desperate
plunges, and I always dodging them, more amused than frightened,
well knowing that when his sober senses returned, he would laugh at
his own drunken folly. At length I observed the mistress standing by
the yard fence, watching our half-serious, half-comical manoeuvres.
Shooting past him, I ran directly to her. Epps, on discovering her,
did not follow. He remained about the field an hour or more, during
which time I stood by the mistress, having related the particulars of
what had taken place. Now, *she* was aroused again, denouncing her
husband and Patsey about equally. Finally, Epps came towards the
house, by this time nearly sober, walking demurely, with his hand
behind his back, and attempting to look as innocent as a child.

As he approached, nevertheless, Mistress Epps began to berate
him roundly, heaping upon him many rather disrespectful epithets,
and demanding for what reason he had attempted to cut my throat.

Epps made wondrous strange of it all, and to my surprise, swore by all the saints in the calendar he had not spoken to me that day.

"Platt, you lying nigger, *have* I?" was his brazen appeal to me.

It is not safe to contradict a master, even by the assertion of a truth. So I was silent, and when he entered the house I returned to the field, and the affair was never after alluded to.

Shortly after this time a circumstance occurred that came nigh divulging the secret of my real name and history, which I had so long and carefully concealed, and upon which I was convinced depended my final escape. Soon after he purchased me, Epps asked me if I could write and read, and on being informed that I had received some instruction in those branches of education, he assured me, with emphasis, if he ever caught me with a book, or with pen and ink, he would give me a hundred lashes. He said he wanted me to understand that he bought "niggers" to work and not to educate. He never inquired a word of my past life, or from whence I came. The mistress, however, cross-examined me frequently about Washington, which she supposed was my native city, and more than once remarked that I did not talk nor act like the other "niggers," and she was sure I had seen more of the world than I admitted.

My great object always was to invent means of getting a letter secretly into the post-office, directed to some of my friends or family at the North. The difficulty of such an achievement cannot be comprehended by one unacquainted with the severe restrictions imposed upon me. In the first place, I was deprived of pen, ink, and paper. In the second place, a slave cannot leave his plantation without a pass, nor will a post-master mail a letter for one without written instructions from his owner. I was in slavery nine years, and always watchful and on the alert, before I met with the good fortune of obtaining a sheet of paper. While Epps was in New-Orleans, one winter, disposing of his cotton, the mistress sent me to Holmesville, with an order for several articles, and among the rest a quantity of foolscap. I appropriated a sheet, concealing it in the cabin, under the board on which I slept.

After various experiments I succeeded in making ink, by boiling white maple bark, and with a feather plucked from the wing of a duck, manufactured a pen. When all were asleep in the cabin, by the light of the coals, lying upon my plank couch, I managed to complete a somewhat lengthy epistle. It was directed to an old acquaintance at Sandy Hill, stating my condition, and urging him to take measures to restore me to liberty. This letter I kept a long time, contriving measures by which it could be safely deposited in the post-office. At length, a low fellow, by the name of Armsby, hitherto a stranger, came into the neighborhood, seeking a situation as overseer. He applied to Epps, and was about the plantation for several days. He next went over to Shaw's, near by, and remained with him several weeks. Shaw was generally surrounded by such worthless characters, being himself noted as a gambler and unprincipled man. He had made a wife of his slave Charlotte, and a brood of young mulattoes were growing up in his house. Armsby became so much reduced at last, that he was compelled to labor with the slaves. A white man working in the field is a rare and unusual spectacle on Bayou Boeuf. I improved every opportunity of cultivating his acquaintance privately, desiring to obtain his confidence so far as to be willing to intrust the letter to his keeping. He visited Marksville repeatedly, he informed me, a town some twenty miles distant, and there, I proposed to myself, the letter should be mailed.

Carefully deliberating on the most proper manner of approaching him on the subject, I concluded finally to ask him simply if he would deposit a letter for me in the Marksville post-office the next time he visited that place, without disclosing to him that the letter was written, or any of the particulars it contained; for I had fears that he might betray me, and knew that some inducement must be held out to him of a pecuniary nature, before it would be safe to confide in him. As late as one o'clock one night I stole noiselessly from my cabin, and crossing the field to Shaw's, found him sleeping on the piazza. I had but a few picayunes—the proceeds of my fiddling performances, but all I had in the world I promised him if he would do me the favor required. I begged him not to expose me if he could not grant the request. He assured me, upon his honor, he would deposit it in the Marksville post-office, and that he would keep it an inviolable secret forever. Though the letter was in my pocket at the time, I dared not then deliver it to him, but stating I would have it written in a day or two, bade him good night, and returned to my cabin. It was impossible for me to expel the suspicions I entertained, and all night I lay awake, revolving in my mind the safest course to pursue. I was willing to risk a great deal to accomplish my purpose, but should the letter by any means fall into the hands of Epps, it would be a death-blow to my aspiration. I was "perplexed in the extreme."

My suspicions were well-founded, as the sequel demonstrated. The next day but one, while scraping cotton in the field, Epps seated himself on the line fence between Shaw's plantation and his own, in such a position as to overlook the scene of our labors. Presently Armsby made his appearance, and, mounting the fence, took a seat beside him. They remained two or three hours, all of which time I was in an agony of apprehension.

That night, while broiling my bacon, Epps entered the cabin with his rawhide in his hand.

"Well, boy," said he, "I understand I've got a lamed nigger, that writes letter, and tries to get white fellows to mail 'em. Wonder if you know who he is?"

My worst fears were realized, and although it may not be considered entirely creditable, even under the circumstances, yet a resort to duplicity and downright falsehood was the only refuge that presented itself.

"Don't know nothing about it, Master Epps," I answered him, assuming an air of ignorance and surprise; "Don't know nothing at all about it, sir."

"Wan't you over to Shaw's the night before last?" he inquired.

"No, master," was the reply.

"Hav'nt you asked that fellow, Armsby, to mail a letter for you at Marksville?"

"Why, Lord, master, I never spoke three words to him in all my life. I don't know what you mean."

"Well," he continued, "Armsby told me to-day the devil was

among my niggers; that I had one that needed close watching or he would run away; and when I axed him why, he said you come over to Shaw's, and waked him up in the night, and wanted him to carry a letter to Marksville. What have you got to say to that, ha?"

"All I've got to say, master," I replied, "is, there is no truth in it. How could I write a letter without any ink or paper? There is nobody I want to write to, 'cause I haint got no friends living as I know of. That Armsby is a lying, drunken fellow, they say, and nobody believes him anyway. You know I always tell the truth, and that I never go off the plantation without a pass. Now, master, I can see what that Armsby is after, plain enough. Did'nt he want you to hire him for an overseer?"

"Yes, he wanted me to hire him," answered Epps.

"That's it," said I, "he wants to make you believe we're all going to run away, and then he thinks you'll hire an overseer to watch us. He just made that story out of whole cloth, 'cause he wants to get a situation. It's all a lie, master, you may depend on't."

Epps mused awhile, evidently impressed with the plausibility of my theory, and exclaimed,

"I'm d—d, Platt, if I don't believe you tell the truth. He must take me for a soft, to think he can come it over me with them kind of yarns, musn't he? Maybe he thinks he can fool me; maybe he thinks I don't know nothing—can't take care of my own niggers, eh! Soft soap old Epps, eh! Ha, ha, ha! D—n Armsby! Set the dogs on him, Platt," and with many other comments descriptive of Armsby's general character, and his capability of taking care of his own business, and attending to his own "niggers," Master Epps left the cabin. As soon as he was gone I threw the letter in the fire, and, with a desponding and despairing heart, beheld the epistle which had cost me so much anxiety and thought, and which I fondly hoped would have been my forerunner to the land of freedom, writhe and shrivel on its bed of coals, and dissolve into smoke and ashes. Armsby, the treacherous wretch, was driven from Shaw's plantation not long subsequently, much to my relief, for I feared he might renew his conversation, and perhaps induce Epps to credit him.

I knew not now whither to look for deliverance. Hopes sprang up in my heart only to be crushed and blighted. The summer of my life was passing away; I felt I was growing prematurely old; that a few years more, and toil, and grief, and the poisonous miasmas of the swamps would accomplish their work upon me—would consign me to the grave's embrace, to moulder and be forgotten. Repelled, betrayed, cut off from the hope of succor, I could only prostrate myself upon the earth and groan in unutterable anguish. The hope of rescue was the only light that cast a ray of comfort on my heart. That was now flickering, faint and low; another breath of disappointment would extinguish it altogether, leaving me to grope in midnight darkness to the end of life.

A Whole Race Begins to Read

BOOKER T. WASHINGTON

I had the feeling that to get into a schoolhouse and study would be about the same as getting into paradise.

Booker Taliaferro Washington was born into slavery in 1856. Upon emancipation, his intense struggle to obtain literacy against great odds formed his opinion on the value of education, and led him to walk five hundred miles to college at Hampton Institute. After several teaching positions, he ultimately founded Tuskegee Institute, now Tuskegee University, in Alabama. His focus on African Americans obtaining agricultural and other industrial skills famously clashed with the views of intellectual W. E. B. Du Bois in how to obtain racial progress.

In this passage from his autobiography, *Up from Slavery*, he takes us back to his early childhood on a plantation in Virginia and then to that historic moment of exhilaration mixed with trepidation when "it was a whole race trying to go to school."

was born a slave on a plantation in Franklin County, Virginia. I am not quite sure of the exact place or exact date of my birth, but at any rate I suspect I must have been born somewhere and at some time. As nearly as I have been able to learn, I was born near a cross-roads post-office called Hale's Ford, and the year was 1858 or 1859. I do not know the month or the day. The earliest impressions I can now recall are of the plantation and the slave quarters—the latter being the part of the plantation where the slaves had their cabins.

My life had its beginning in the midst of the most miserable, desolate, and discouraging surroundings. This was so, however, not because my owners were especially cruel, for they were not, as compared with many others. I was born in a typical log cabin, about fourteen by sixteen feet square. In this cabin I lived with my mother and a brother and sister till after the Civil War, when we were all declared free.

Of my ancestry I know almost nothing. In the slave quarters, and even later, I heard whispered conversations among the coloured people of the tortures which the slaves, including, no doubt, my ancestors on my mother's side, suffered in the middle passage of the slave ship while being conveyed from Africa to America. I have been unsuccessful in securing any information that would throw any accurate light upon the history of my family beyond my mother. She, I remember, had a half-brother and a half-sister. In the days of slavery not very much attention was given to family history and family records—that is, black family records. My mother, I suppose, attracted the attention of a purchaser who was afterward my owner and hers. Her addition to the slave family attracted about as much attention as the purchase of a new horse or cow.

Of my father I know even less than of my mother. I do not even know his name. I have heard reports to the effect that he was a white man who lived on one of the near-by plantations. Whoever he was, I never heard of his taking the least interest in me or providing in any way for my rearing. But I do not find especial fault with him. He was simply another unfortunate victim of the institution which the Nation unhappily had engrafted upon it at that time. . . .

The early years of my life, which were spent in the little cabin, were not very different from those of thousands of other slaves. My mother, of course, had little time in which to give attention to the training of her children during the day. She snatched a few moments for our care in the early morning before her work began, and at night after the day's work was done. One of my earliest recollections is that of my mother cooking a chicken late at night, and awakening her children for the purpose of feeding them. How or where she got it I do not know. I presume, however, it was procured from our owner's farm. Some people may call this theft. If such a thing were to happen now, I should condemn it as theft myself. But taking place at the time it did, and for the reason that it did, no one could ever make me believe that my mother was guilty of thieving. She was simply a victim of the system of slavery. I cannot remember having slept in a bed until after our family was declared free by the Emancipation Proclamation. Three children—John, my older brother, Amanda, my sister, and myself—had a pallet on the dirt floor, or, to be more correct, we slept in and on a bundle of filthy rags laid upon the dirt floor.

I was asked not long ago to tell something about the sports and pastimes that I engaged in during my youth. Until that question was asked it had never occurred to me that there was no period of my life that was devoted to play. From the time that I can remember anything, almost every day of my life has been occupied in some kind of labour; though I think I would now be a more useful man if I had had time for sports. . . .

I had no schooling whatever while I was a slave, though I remember on several occasions I went as far as the schoolhouse door with one of my young mistresses to carry her books. The picture of several dozen boys and girls in a schoolroom engaged in study made a deep impression upon me, and I had the feeling that to get into a schoolhouse and study in this way would be about the same as getting into paradise.

So far as I can now recall, the first knowledge that I got of the fact that we were slaves, and that freedom of the slaves was being discussed, was early one morning before day, when I was awakened by my mother kneeling over her children and fervently praying that Lincoln and his armies might be successful, and that one day she and her children might be free. In this connection I have never been able to understand how the slaves throughout the South, completely ignorant as were the masses so far as books or newspapers were concerned, were able to keep themselves so accurately and completely informed about the great National questions that were agitating the country. From the time that Garrison, Lovejoy, and others began to agitate for freedom, the slaves throughout the South kept in close touch with the progress of the movement. Though I was a mere child during the preparation for the Civil War and during the war itself, I now recall the many late-at-night whispered discussions that I heard my mother and the other slaves on the plantation indulge in. These discussions showed that they understood the situation, and that they kept themselves informed of events by what was termed the "grape-vine" telegraph.

During the campaign when Lincoln was first a candidate for the Presidency, the slaves on our far-off plantation, miles from any rail-road or large city or daily newspaper, knew what the issues involved were. When war was begun between the North and the South, every slave on our plantation felt and knew that, though other issues were discussed, the primal one was that of slavery. Even the most ignorant members of my race on the remote plantations felt in their hearts, with a certainty that admitted of no doubt, that the freedom of the slaves would be the one great result of the war, if the Northern armies conquered. Every success of the Federal armies and every defeat of the Confederate forces was watched with the keenest and most intense interest. Often the slaves got knowledge of the results of great battles before the white people received it. This news was usually gotten from the coloured man who was sent to the post-office for the mail. In our case the post-office was about three miles from the plantation, and the mail came once or twice a week. The man who was sent to the office would linger about the place long enough to get the drift of the conversation from the group of white people who naturally congregated there, after receiving their mail, to discuss the latest news. The mail-carrier on his way back to our master's house would as naturally retail the news that he had secured among the slaves, and in this way they often heard of important events before the white people at the "big house," as the master's house was called. . . .

One may get the idea, from what I have said, that there was bitter feeling toward the white people on the part of my race, because of the fact that most of the white population was away fighting in a war which would result in keeping the Negro in slavery if the South was successful. In the case of the slaves on our place this was not true, and it was not true of any large portion of the slave population in the South where the Negro was treated with anything like decency. During the Civil War one of my young masters was killed, and two were severely wounded. I recall the feeling of sorrow which existed among the slaves when they heard of the deal of "Mars' Billy." It was no sham sorrow, but real. Some of the slaves had nursed "Mars' Billy"; others had played with him when he was a child. "Mars' Billy" had begged for mercy in the case of others when the overseer or master was thrashing them. The sorrow in the slave quarter was only second to that in the "big house." When the two young masters were brought home wounded, the sympathy of the slaves was shown in many ways. They were just as anxious to assist in the nursing as the family relatives of the wounded. Some of the slaves would even beg for the privilege of sitting up at night to nurse their wounded masters. This tenderness and sympathy on the part of those held in bondage was a result of their kindly and generous nature. In order to defend and protect the women and children who were left on the plantations when the white males went to war, the slaves would have laid down their lives. The slave who was selected to sleep in the "big house" during the absence of the males was considered to have the place of honour. Any one attempting to harm "young Mistress" or "old Mistress" during the night would have had to cross the dead body of the slave to do so. I do not know how many have noticed it, but I think that it will be found to be true that there are few instances, either in slavery or freedom, in which a member of my race has been known to betray a specific trust.

As a rule, not only did the members of my race entertain no feelings of bitterness against the whites before and during the war, but there are many instances of Negroes tenderly caring for their former masters and mistresses who for some reason have become poor and dependent since the war. I know of instances where the former masters of slaves have for years been supplied with money by their former slaves to keep them from suffering. I have known of still other cases in which the former slaves have assisted in the education of the descendants of their former owners. I know of a case on a large plantation in the South in which a young white man, the son of the former owner of the estate, has become so reduced in purse and self-control by reason of drink that he is a pitiable creature; and yet, notwithstanding the poverty of the coloured people themselves on this plantation, they have for years supplied this young white man with the necessities of life. One sends him a little coffee or sugar, another a little meat, and so on. Nothing that the coloured people possess is too good for the son of "ole Mars' Tom," who will perhaps never be permitted to suffer while any remain on the place who knew directly or indirectly of "old Mars' Tom."

I have said that there are few instances of a member of my race betraying a specific trust. One of the best illustrations of this which I know of is in the case of an ex-slave from Virginia whom I met not long ago in a little town in the state of Ohio. I found that this man had made a contract with his master, two or three years previous to the Emancipation Proclamation, to the effect that the slave was to be permitted to buy himself, by paying so much per year for his body; and while he was paying for himself, he was permitted to labour where and for whom he pleased. Finding that he could secure better wages in Ohio, he went there. When freedom came, he was still in debt to his master some three hundred dollars. Notwithstanding that the Emancipation Proclamation freed him from any obligation to his master, this black man walked the great portion of the distance back to where his old master lived in Virginia, and placed the last dollar, with interest, in his hands. In talking to me about this, the man told me that he knew that he did not have to pay the debt, but that he had given his word to his master and his word he had never broken. He felt that he could not enjoy his freedom till he had fulfilled his promise.

From some things that I have said one may get the idea that some of the slaves did not want freedom. This is not true. I have never seen one who did not want to be free, or who would return to slavery. . . .

Finally the war closed, and the day of freedom came. It was a momentous and eventful day to all upon our plantation. We had been expecting it. Freedom was in the air, and had been for months. Deserting soldiers returning to their homes were to be seen every day. Others who had been discharged, or whose regiments had been paroled, were constantly passing near our place. The "grape-vine telegraph" was kept busy night and day. The news and mutterings of great events were swiftly carried from one plantation to another. In the fear of "Yankee" intrusions, the silverware and other valuables were taken from the "big house," buried in the woods, and guarded by trusted slaves. Woe be to any one who would have attempted to disturb the buried treasure. The slave would give the Yankee soldiers food, drink, clothing—anything but that which had been specifically intrusted to their care and honour.

As the great day drew nearer, there was more singing in the slave quarters than usual. It was bolder, had more ring, and lasted later into the night. Most of the verses of the plantation songs had some reference to freedom. True, they had sung those same verses before, but they had been careful to explain that the "freedom" in these songs referred to the next world, and had no connection with life in this world. Now they gradually threw off the mask, and were not afraid to let it be known that the "freedom" in their songs meant freedom of the body in this world. The night before the eventful day, word was sent to the slave quarters to the effect that something unusual was going to take place at the "big house" the next morning. There was little, if any, sleep that night. All was excitement and expectancy. Early the next morning word was sent to all the slaves, old and young, to gather at the house. In company with my mother, brother, and sister, and a large number of other slaves, I went to the master's house. All of our master's family were either standing or seated on the veranda of the house, where they could see what was to take place and hear what was said. There was a feeling of deep interest, or perhaps sadness, on their faces, but not bitterness. As I now recall the impression they made upon me, they did not at the moment seem to be sad because of the loss of property, but rather because of parting with those whom they had reared and who were in many ways very close to them. The most distinct thing that I now recall in connection with the scene was that some man who seemed to be a stranger (a United States officer, I presume) made a little speech and then read a rather long paper—the Emancipation Proclamation, I think. After the reading we were told that we were all free, and could go when and where we pleased. My mother, who was standing by my side, leaned over and kissed her children, while tears of joy ran down her cheeks. She explained to us what it all meant, that this was the day for which she had been so long praying, but fearing that she would never live to see. . . .

Boyhood Days

After the coming of freedom there were two points upon which practically all the people on our place were agreed, and I find that this was generally true throughout the South: that they must change their names, and that they must leave the old plantation for at least a few days or weeks in order that they might really feel sure that they were free.

In some way a feeling got among the coloured people that it was far from proper for them to bear the surname of their former owners, and a great many of them took other surnames. This was one of the first signs of freedom. When they were slaves, a coloured person was simply called "John" or "Susan." There was seldom occasion for more than the use of the one name. If "John" or "Susan" belonged to a white man by the name of "Hatcher," sometimes he was called "John Hatcher," or as often "Hatcher's John." But there was a feeling that "John Hatcher" or "Hatcher's John" was not the proper title by which to denote a freeman; and so in many cases "John Hatcher" was changed to "John S. Lincoln" or "John S. Sherman," the initial "S" standing for no name, it being simply a part of what the coloured man proudly called his "entitles."

As I have stated, most of the coloured people left the old plantation for a short while at least, so as to be sure, it seemed, that they could leave and try their freedom on to see how it felt. After they had remained away for a time, many of the older slaves, especially, returned to their old homes and made some kind of contract with their former owners by which they remained on the estate.

My mother's husband, who was the stepfather of my brother John and myself, did not belong to the same owners as did my mother. In fact, he seldom came to our plantation. I remember seeing him there perhaps once a year, that being around Christmas time. In some way, during the war, by running away and following the Federal soldiers, it seems, he found his way into the new state of West Virginia. As soon as freedom was declared, he sent for my mother to come to the Kanawha Valley, in West Virginia. At that time a journey from Virginia over the mountains to West Virginia was rather a tedious and in some cases a painful undertaking. What little clothing and few household goods we had were placed in a cart, but the children walked the greater portion of the distance, which was several hundred miles.

I do not think any of us ever had been very far from the plantation, and the taking of a long journey into another state was quite an event. The parting from our former owners and the members of our own race on the plantation was a serious occasion. From the time of our parting till their death we kept up a correspondence with the older members of the family, and in later years we have kept in touch with those who were the younger members. We were several weeks making the trip, and most of the time we slept in the open air and did our cooking over a log fire out-of-doors. One night I recall that we camped near an abandoned log cabin, and my mother decided to build a fire in that for cooking, and afterward to make a "pallet" on the floor for our sleeping. Just as the fire had gotten well started a large black snake fully a yard and a half long dropped down the chimney and ran out on the floor. Of course, we at once abandoned that cabin. Finally we reached our destination—a little town called Malden, which is about five miles from Charleston, the present capital of the state.

At that time salt-mining was the great industry in that part of West Virginia, and the little town of Malden was right in the midst of the salt-furnaces. My stepfather had already secured a job at a salt-furnace, and he had also secured a little cabin for us to live in. Our new house was no better than the one we had left on the old plantation in Virginia. In fact, in one respect it was worse. Notwithstanding the poor condition of our plantation cabin, we were at all times sure of pure air. Our new home was in the midst of a cluster of cabins crowded closely together, and as there were no sanitary regulations, the filth about the cabins was often intolerable. Some of our neighbours were coloured people, and some were the poorest and most ignorant and degraded white people. It was a motley mixture. Drinking, gambling, quarrels, fights, and shockingly immoral practices were frequent. All who lived in the little town were in one way or another connected with the salt business. Though I was a mere child, my stepfather put me and my brother at work in one of the furnaces. Often I began work as early as four o'clock in the morning.

The first thing I ever learned in the way of book knowledge was while working in this salt-furnace. Each salt-packer had his barrels marked with a certain number. The number allotted to my stepfather was "18." At the close of the day's work the boss of the packers would come around and put "18" on each of our barrels, and I soon learned to recognize that figure wherever I saw it, and after a while got to the point where I could make that figure, though I knew nothing about any other figures or letters.

From the time that I can remember having any thoughts about anything, I recall that I had an intense longing to learn to read. I determined, when quite a small child, that, if I accomplished nothing else in life, I would in some way get enough education to enable me to read common books and newspapers. Soon after we got settled in some manner in our new cabin in West Virginia, I induced my mother to get hold of a book for me. How or where she got it I do not know, but in some way she procured an old copy of Webster's "blue-back" spelling-book, which contained the alphabet, followed by such meaningless words as "ab," "ba," "ca," "da." I began at once to devour this book, and I think that it was the first one I ever had in my hands. I had learned from somebody that the way to begin to read was to learn the alphabet, so I tried in all the ways I could think of to learn it, —all of course without a teacher, for I could find no one to teach me. At that time there was not a single member of my race anywhere near us who could read, and I was too timid to approach any of the white people. In some way, within a few weeks, I mastered the greater portion of the alphabet. In all my efforts to learn to read my mother shared fully my ambition, and sympathized with me and aided me in every way that she could. Though she was totally ignorant, so far as mere book knowledge was concerned, she had high ambitions for her children, and a large fund of good, hard, common sense which seemed to enable her to meet and master every situation. If I have anything in life worth attention, I feel sure that I inherited the disposition from my mother.

In the midst of my struggles and longing for an education, a young coloured boy who had learned to read in the state of Ohio came to Malden. As soon as the coloured people found out that he could read, a newspaper was secured, and at the close of nearly every day's work this young man would be surrounded by a group of men and women who were anxious to hear him read the news contained in the papers. How I used to envy this man! He seemed to me to be the one young man in all the world who ought to be satisfied with his attainments.

About this time the question of having some kind of a school opened for the coloured children in the village began to be discussed by members of the race. As it would be the first school for Negro children that had ever been opened in that part of Virginia, it was, of course, to be a great event, and the discussion excited the widest interest. The most perplexing question was where to find a teacher. The young man from Ohio who had learned to read the papers was considered, but his age was against him. In the midst of the discussion about a teacher, another young coloured man from Ohio, who had been a soldier, in some way found his way into town. It was soon learned that he possessed considerable education, and he was engaged by the coloured people to teach their first school. As yet no free schools had been started for coloured people in that section, hence each family agreed to pay a certain amount per month, with the understanding that the teacher was to "board 'round"—that is, spend a day with each family. This was not bad for the teacher, for each family tried to provide the very best on the day the teacher was to be its guest. I recall that I looked forward with an anxious appetite to the "teacher's day" at our little cabin.

This experience of a whole race beginning to go to school for the first time, presents one of the most interesting studies that has ever occurred in connection with the development of any race. Few people who were not right in the midst of the scenes can form any exact idea of the intense desire which the people of my race showed for an education. As I have stated, it was a whole race trying to go to school. Few were too young, and none too old, to make the attempt to learn. As fast as any kind of teachers could be secured, not only were day-schools filled, but night-schools as well. The great ambition of the older people was to try to learn to read the Bible before they died. With this end in view, men and women who were fifty or seventy-five years old would often be found in the night-school. Sunday-schools were formed soon after freedom, but the principal book studied in the Sunday-school was the spelling book. Day-school, night-school, Sunday-school, were always crowded, and often many had to be turned away for want of room.

The opening of the school in the Kanawha Valley, however,

brought to me one of the keenest disappointments that I ever experienced. I had been working in a salt-furnace for several months, and my stepfather had discovered that I had a financial value, and so, when the school opened, he decided that he could not spare me from my work. This decision seemed to cloud my every ambition. The disappointment was made all the more severe by reason of the fact that my place of work was where I could see the happy children passing to and from school, morning and afternoons. Despite this disappointment, however, I determined that I would learn something, anyway. I applied myself with greater earnestness than ever to the mastering of what was in the "blue-back" speller.

My mother sympathized with me in my disappointment, and sought to comfort me in all the ways she could, and to help me find a way to learn. After a while I succeeded in making arrangements with the teacher to give me some lessons at night, after the day's work was done. These night lessons were so welcome that I think I learned more at night than the other children did during the day. My own experiences in the night-school gave me faith in the night-school idea, with which, in after years, I had to do both at Hampton and Tuskegee. But my boyish heart was still set upon going to the day-school, and I let no opportunity slip to push my case. Finally I won, and was permitted to go to the school in the day for a few months, with the understanding that I was to rise early in the morning and work in the furnace till nine o'clock, and return immediately after school closed in the afternoon for at least two more hours of work.

The schoolhouse was some distance from the furnace, and as I had to work till nine o'clock, and the school opened at nine, I found myself in a difficulty. School would always be begun before I reached it, and sometimes my class had recited. To get around this difficulty I yielded to a temptation for which most people, I suppose, will condemn me; but since it is a fact, I might as well state it. I have great faith in the power and influence of facts. It is seldom that anything is permanently gained by holding back a fact. There was a large clock in a little office in the furnace. This clock, of course, all the hundred or more workmen depended upon to regulate their hours of beginning and ending the day's work. I got the idea that the way for me to reach school on time was to move the clock hands from half-past eight up to the nine o'clock mark. This I found myself doing morning after morning, till the furnace "boss" discovered that something was wrong, and locked the clock in a case. I did not mean to inconvenience anybody. I simply meant to reach that schoolhouse in time.

When, however, I found myself at the school for the first time, I also found myself confronted with two other difficulties. In the first place, I found that all of the other children wore hats or caps on their heads, and I had neither hat nor cap. In fact, I do not remember that up to the time of going to school I had ever worn any kind of covering upon my head, nor do I recall that either I or anybody else had even thought anything about the need of covering for my head. But, of course, when I saw how all the other boys were dressed, I began to feel quite uncomfortable. As usual, I put the case before my mother, and she explained to me that she had no money with which to buy a "store hat," which was a rather new institution at that time among the members of my race and was considered quite the thing for young and old to own, but that she would find a way to help me out of the difficulty. She accordingly got two pieces of "homespun" (jeans) and sewed them together, and I was soon the proud possessor of my first cap.

The lesson that my mother taught me in this has always remained with me, and I have tried as best I could to teach it to others. I have always felt proud, whenever I think of the incident, that my mother had strength of character enough not to be led into the temptation of seeming to be that which she was not—of trying to impress my schoolmates and others with the fact that she was able to buy me a "store hat" when she was not. I have always felt proud that she refused to go into debt for that which she did not have the money to pay for. Since that time I have owned many kinds of caps and hats, but never one of which I have felt so proud as of the cap made of the two pieces of cloth sewed together by my mother. I have noted the fact, but without satisfaction, I need not add, that several of the boys who began their careers with "store hats" and who were my

schoolmates and used to join in the sport that was made of me because I had only a "homespun" cap, have ended their careers in the
penitentiary, while others are not able now to buy any kind of hat.

My second difficulty was with regard to my name, or rather
a name. From the time when I could remember anything, I had
been called simply "Booker." Before going to school it had never
occurred to me that it was needful or appropriate to have an additional name. When I heard the school-roll called, I noticed that all
of the children had at least two names, and some of them indulged
in what seemed to me the extravagance of having three. I was in
deep perplexity, because I knew that the teacher would demand of
me at least two names, and I had only one. By the time the occasion
came for the enrolling of my name, an idea occurred to me which
I thought would make me equal to the situation; and so, when the
teacher asked me what my full name was, I calmly told him "Booker
Washington," as if I had been called by that name all my life; and
by that name I have since been known. Later in my life I found
that my mother had given me the name of "Booker Taliaferro" soon
after I was born, but in some way that part of my name seemed to
disappear and for a long while was forgotten, but as soon as I found
out about it I revived it, and made my full name "Booker Taliaferro
Washington." I think there are not many men in country who have
had the privilege of naming themselves in the way that I have.

More than once I have tried to picture myself in the position of
a boy or man with an honoured and distinguished ancestry which
I could trace back through a period of hundreds of years, and who
had not only inherited a name, but fortune and a proud family
homestead; and yet I have sometimes had the feeling that if I had
inherited these, and had been a member of a more popular race, I
should have been inclined to yield to the temptation of depending
upon my ancestry and my colour to do that for me which I should
do for myself. Years ago I resolved that because I had no ancestry
myself I would leave a record of which my children would be proud,
and which might encourage them to still higher effort.

The Negro in Literature and Art

W. E. B. DU BOIS

We can afford the Truth, white folk today cannot. As it is
now we are handing everything over to a white jury. If a
colored man wants to publish a book, he has got to get a
white publisher and a white newspaper to say it is great.

William Edward Burghardt Du Bois was born in 1868 in Great Bar-
rington, Massachusetts. The first African American to earn a doctorate
from Harvard, he became one of the most important civil rights activists
of the early 1900s. In 1909, Du Bois was a cofounder of the National
Association for the Advancement of Colored People and served as the
editor of the NAACP magazine, the *Crisis*. Known for his classic book of
essays, *The Souls of Black Folk*, Du Bois also wrote three autobiographies. A proponent of Pan-Africanism, he and his wife, Shirley Graham
Du Bois, relocated to Ghana, where he died in 1963 at the age of ninety-
five on the eve of the March on Washington for Jobs and Freedom.

What follows is a survey Du Bois published of Black literature from
early Egyptian civilization to the time of its writing, in 1913. The
ending section is taken from a separate essay he wrote on a similar
subject—"Criteria of Negro Art," for the *Crisis* in 1926—and still reso-
nates in the world of publishing today.

The Negro is primarily an artist. The usual way of putting this is to speak disdainfully of his sensuous nature. This means that the only race which has held at bay the life destroying forces of the tropics, has gained therefrom in some slight compensation a sense of beauty, particularly for sound and color, which characterizes the race. The Negro blood which flowed in the veins of many of the mightiest of the Pharaohs accounts for much of Egyptian art, and indeed, Egyptian civilization owes much in its origins to the development of the large strain of Negro blood which manifested itself in every grade of Egyptian society.

Semitic civilization also had its Negroid influences, and these continually turn toward art as in the case of Nosseyeb, one of the five great poets of Damascus under the Ommiades. It was therefore not to be wondered at that in modern days one of the greatest of modern literatures, the Russian, should have been founded by Pushkin, the grandson of a full blooded Negro, and that among the painters of Spain was the mulatto slave, Gomez. Back of all this development by way of contact, comes the artistic sense of the indigenous Negro as shown in the stone figures of Sherbro, the bronzes of Benin, the marvelous handwork in iron and other metals which has characterized the Negro race so long that archeologists today, with less and less hesitation, are ascribing the discovery of the welding of iron to the Negro race. . . .

The expression in words of the tragic experiences of the Negro race is to be found in various places. First, of course, there are those, like Harriet Beecher Stowe, who wrote from without the race. Then there are black men like Es-Sadi, who wrote the Epic of the Sudan, in Arabic, that great history of the fall of the greatest of Negro empires, the Songhay. In America the literary expression of Negroes has had a regular development. As early as the eighteenth century, and even before the Revolutionary War the first voices of Negro authors were heard in the United States.

Phyllis [*sic*] Wheatley, the black poetess, was easily the pioneer, her first poems appearing in 1773, and other editions in 1774 and 1793. Her earliest poem was in memory of George Whitefield. She was followed by the Negro, Olaudah Equiano—known by his English name of Gustavus Vassa—whose autobiography of 350 pages, published in 1787, was the beginning of that long series of personal appeals of which Booker T. Washington's *Up from Slavery* is the latest. Benjamin Banneker's almanacs represented the first scientific work of American Negroes, and began to be issued in 1792.

Coming now to the first decades of the nineteenth century we find some essays on freedom by the African Society of Boston, and an apology for the new Negro church formed in Philadelphia. Paul Cuffe, disgusted with America, wrote an early account of Sierra Leone, while the celebrated Lemuel Haynes, ignoring the race question, dipped deeply into the New England theological controversy about 1815. In 1829 came the first full-voiced, almost hysterical, protest against slavery and the color line in David Walker's *Appeal* which aroused Southern legislatures to action. This was followed by the earliest Negro conventions which issued interesting minutes, and a strong appeal against disfranchisement in Pennsylvania.

In 1840 some strong writers began to appear. Henry Highland Garnet and J. W. C. Pennington preached powerful sermons and gave some attention to Negro history in their pamphlets; R. B. Lewis made a more elaborate attempt at Negro history. Whitfield's poems appeared in 1846, and William Wells Brown began a career of writing which lasted from 1847 until after the war. In 1845 Douglass' autobiography made its first appearance, destined to run through endless editions up until the last in 1893. Moreover it was in 1841 that the first Negro magazine appeared in America, edited by George Hogarth and published by the A. M. E. Church.

In the fifties Williams Wells Brown published his *Three Years in Europe*; James Whitfield published further poems, and a new poet arose in the person of Frances E. W. Harper, a woman of no little ability who died lately; Martin R. Delaney and William Nell wrote further of Negro history, Nell especially making valuable contributions to the history of the Negro soldiers. Three interesting biographies were added to this decade to the growing number: Josiah Henson, Samuel G. Ward and Samuel Northrop [*sic*]; while Catto, leaving general history, came down to the better known history of the Negro church.

In the sixties slave narratives multiplied, like that of Linda Brent, while two studies of Africa based on actual visits were made by Robert Campbell and Dr. Alexander Crummell; William Douglass and Bishop Daniel Payne continued the history of the Negro church, while William Wells Brown carried forward his work in general Negro history. In this decade, too, Bishop Tanner began his work in Negro theology.

Most of the Negro talent in the seventies was taken up in politics; the older men like Bishop Wayman wrote of their experiences; William Wells Brown wrote the *Rising Son*, and Sojourner Truth added her story to the slave narratives. A new poet arose in the person of A. A. Whitman, while James M. Trotter was the first to take literary note of the musical ability of his race. Indeed this section might have been begun by some reference to the music and folklore of the Negro race; the music contained much primitive poetry and the folklore was one of the great contributions to American civilization.

In the eighties there are signs of unrest and different conflicting streams of thought. On the one hand the rapid growth of the Negro church is shown by the writers on church subjects like Moore and Wayman. The historical spirit was especially strong. Still wrote of the *Underground Railroad*; Simmons issued his interesting biographical dictionary, and the greatest historian of the race appeared when George W. Williams issued his two-volume history of the *Negro Race in America*. The political turmoil was reflected in Langston's *Freedom and Citizenship*, Fortune's *Black and White*, and Straker's *New South*, and found its bitterest arraignment in Turner's pamphlets; but with all this went other new thought; a black man published his *First Greek Lessons*, Bishop Payne issued his *Treatise on Domestic Education*, and Steward studied Liberia.

In the nineties came histories, essays, novels and poems, together with biographies and social studies. The history was represented by

Payne's *History of the A. M. E. Church*, Hood's *History of the A. M. E. Zion Church*, Anderson's sketch of *Negro Presbyterianism* and Hagood's *Colored Man in the M. E. Church*; general history of the older type by R. L. Perry's *Cushite* and the newer type in Johnson's history, while one of the secret societies found their historian in Brooks; Crogman's essays appeared and Archibald Grimke's biographies. The race question was discussed in Frank Grimke's published sermons, while social studies were made by Penn, Wright, Mossell, Crummell, Majors and others. Most notable, however, was the rise of the Negro novelist and poet with national recognition; Frances Harper was still writing and Griggs began his racial novels, but both of these spoke primarily to the Negro race; on the other hand, Chesnutt's six novels and Dunbar's inimitable works spoke to the whole nation.

Since 1900 the stream of Negro writing has continued. Dunbar has found a worthy successor in the less-known but more carefully cultured Braithwaite; Booker T. Washington has given us his biography and *Story of the Negro*; Kelly Miller's trenchant essays have appeared in book form; Sinclair's *Aftermath of Slavery* has attracted attention, as have the studies made by Atlanta University. . . .

On the whole, the literary output of the American Negro has been both large and creditable, although, of course, comparatively little known; few great names have appeared and only here and there work that could be called first class, but this is not a peculiarity of Negro literature.

The time has not yet come for the great development of American Negro literature. The economic stress is too great and the racial persecution too bitter to allow the leisure and the poise for which literature calls. On the other hand, never in the world has a richer mass of material been accumulated by a people than that which the Negroes possess today and are becoming conscious of. Slowly but surely they are developing artists of technic who will be able to use this material. The nation does not notice this for everything touching the Negro is banned by magazines and publishers unless it takes the form of caricature or bitter attack, or is so thoroughly innocuous as to have no literary flavor. . . . So this sum of accomplishment is but an imperfect implication of what the Negro race is capable of in America and in the world.

Criteria of Negro Art

. . . In all sorts of ways we are hemmed in and our new young artists have got to fight their way to freedom.

The ultimate judge has got to be you and you have got to build yourselves up into that wide judgment, that catholicity of temper which is going to enable the artist to have his widest chance for freedom. We can afford the Truth. White folk today cannot. As it is now we are handing everything over to a white jury. If a colored man wants to publish a book, he has got to get a white publisher and a white newspaper to say it is great; and then you and I say so. We must come to the place where the work of art when it appears is reviewed and acclaimed by our own free and unfettered judgment. And we are going to have a real and valuable and eternal judgment only as we make ourselves free of mind, proud of body and just of soul to all men. . . .

THE POWER

1900–1968

In this era, from the post-Emancipation period through the Civil Rights / Black Power era, writers as diverse as Zora Neale Hurston and Stokely Carmichael had something in common—the relentless pursuit of equality and freedom for all.

Books and Things

ZORA NEALE HURSTON

I took my nerve in my hand and decided to try to
write the story I had been carrying around in me.

Zora Neale Hurston (1891–1960) is one of the most beloved and pre-
eminent African American women writers. Her classic novel, *Their Eyes
Were Watching God*, published in 1937, is still taught in schools and
was made into a television movie in 2005.

Born in Alabama, Hurston grew up in Eatonville, Florida, where she
was influenced by the "tall tales" she heard there. She obtained an
associate degree from Howard University and in 1921 published her
first short story in the school's literary magazine, the *Stylus*. In 1924,
she cofounded the campus newspaper, the *Hilltop*. Hurston went on to
graduate from Barnard College in 1928 and later studied for a PhD in
anthropology from Columbia University.

As a luminary of the Harlem Renaissance of the 1920s, Hurston
was a prolific author of short stories, essays, plays, novels, and an autobiography, *Dust Tracks on a Road*. Published in 1942 and excerpted
here, *Dust Tracks* gives us the author's own story of the challenges and
triumphs of being a Negro writer.

While I was in the research field in 1929, the idea of *Jonah's Gourd Vine* came to me. I had written a few short stories, but the idea of attempting a book seemed so big, that I gazed at it in the quiet of the night, but hid it away from even myself in daylight.

For one thing, it seemed off-key. What I wanted to tell was a story about a man, and from what I had read and heard, Negroes were supposed to write about the Race Problem. I was and am thoroughly sick of the subject. My interest lies in what makes a man or a woman do such-and-so, regardless of his color. It seemed to me that the human beings I met reacted pretty much the same to the same stimuli. Different idioms, yes. Circumstances and conditions having power to influence, yes. Inherent difference, no. But I said to myself that that was not what was expected of me, so I was afraid to tell a story the way I wanted, or rather the way the story told itself to me. So I went on that way for three years.

Something else held my attention for a while. As I told you before, I had been pitched head-foremost into the Baptist Church when I was born. I had heard the singing, the preaching and the prayers. They were a part of me. But on the concert stage, I always heard songs called spirituals sung and applauded as Negro music, and I wondered what would happen if a white audience ever heard a real spiritual. To me, what the Negroes did in Macedonia Baptist Church was finer than anything that any trained composer had done to the folk songs.

I had collected a mass of work songs, blues and spirituals in the course of my years of research. After offering them to two Negro composers and having them refused on the ground that white audiences would not listen to anything but highly arranged spirituals, I decided to see if that was true. I doubted it because I had seen groups of white people in my father's church as early as I could remember. They had come to hear the singing, and certainly there was no distinguished composer in Zion Hope Baptist Church. The congregation just got hold of the tune and arranged as they went along as the spirit moved them. And any musician, I don't care if he stayed at a conservatory until his teeth were gone and he smelled like old-folks, could never even approach what those untrained singers could do. LET THE PEOPLE SING, was and is my motto, and finally I resolved to see what would happen.

So on money I borrowed, I put on a show at the John Golden Theater on January 10, 1932, and tried out my theory. The performance was well received by both the audience and the critics. Because I know that music without motion is not natural with my people, I did not have the singers stand in a stiff group and reach for the high note. I told them to just imagine that they were in Macedonia and go ahead. One critic said that he did not believe that the concert was rehearsed, it looked so natural. I had dramatized a working day on a railroad camp, from the shack-rouser waking up the camp at dawn until the primitive dance in the deep woods at night.

While I did not lose any money, I did not make much. But I am satisfied that I proved my point. I have seen the effects of that concert in all the Negro singing groups since then. Primitive Negro dancing has been given tremendous impetus. Work songs have taken on. In that performance I introduced West Indian songs and dances and they have come to take an important place in America. I am not upset by the fact that others have made something out of the things I pointed out. Rather I am glad if I have called any beauty to the attention of those who can use it.

In May, 1932, the depression did away with money for research so far as I was concerned. So I took my nerve in my hand and decided to try to write the story I had been carrying around in me. Back in my native village, I wrote first *Mules and Men*. That is, I edited the huge mass of material I had, arranged it in some sequence and laid it aside. It was published after my first novel. Mr. Robert Wunsch and Dr. John Rice were both on the faculty of Rollins College, at Winter Park, which is three miles from Eatonville. Dr. Edwin Osgood Grover, Dr. Hamilton Holt, President of Rollins, together with Rice and Wunsch, were interested in me. I gave three folk concerts at the college under their urging.

Then I wrote a short story, "The Gilded Six-Bits," which Bob Wunsch read to his class in creative writing before he sent if off to *Story Magazine*. Thus I came to know Martha Foley and her husband, Whit Burnett, the editors of *Story*. They bought the story and it was published in the August issue, 1933. They never told me, but it is my belief that they did some missionary work among publishers in my behalf, because four publishers wrote me and asked if I had anything of book-length. Mr. Bertram Lippincott, of the J. B. Lippincott Company, was among these. He wrote a gentle-like letter and so I was not afraid of him. Exposing my efforts did not seem so rash to me after reading his letter. I wrote him and said that I was writing a book. Mind you, not the first word was on paper when I wrote him that letter. But the very next week I moved up to Sanford where I was not so much at home as at Eatonville, and could concentrate more and sat down to write *Jonah's Gourd Vine*.

I rented a house with a bed and stove in it for $1.50 a week. I paid two weeks and then my money ran out. My cousin, Willie Lee Hurston, was working and making $3.50 per week, and she always gave me the fifty cents to buy groceries with. In about three months, I finished the book. The problem of getting it typed was then upon me. Municipal Judge S.A.B. Wilkinson asked his secretary, Mildred Knight, if she would not do it for me and wait on the money. I explained to her that the book might not even be taken by Lippincott. I had been working on a hope. She took the manuscript home with her and read it. Then she offered to type it for me. She said, "It is going to be accepted, all right. I'll type it. Even if the first publisher does not take it, somebody will." So between them, they bought the paper and carbon and the book was typed.

I took it down to the American Express office to mail it and found that it cost $1.83 cents to mail, and I did not have it. So I went to see Mrs. John Leonardi, a most capable woman lawyer, and wife of the County Prosecutor. She did not have the money at the moment, but she was the treasurer of the local Daughter Elks. She "borrowed" $2.00 from the treasury and gave it to me to mail my book. That was on October 3, 1933. On October 16, I had an acceptance by wire.

But it did not come so simply as that. I had been hired by the Seminole County Chamber of Commerce to entertain the business district of Sanford with my concert group for that day. I was very glad to get the work, because my landlord was pressing me for the back rent. I now owed $18. I was to receive $25 for the day, so I saw my way clear to pay up my rent, and have a little over. It was not to be that way, however. At eight o'clock of October 16, my landlord came and told me to get out. I told her that I could pay her that day, but she said she didn't believe that I would ever have that much money. No, she preferred the house. So I took my card table and my clothes up to my Uncle Isaiah's house and went off to entertain the city at eleven o'clock. The sound truck went up and down the streets and my boys sang. That afternoon while I was still on the sound truck, a Western Union messenger handed me a wire. Naturally I did not open it there. We were through at three o'clock. The Chamber of Commerce not only paid us, we were all given an order which we could take to any store we wanted and get what we chose. I needed shoes, so I took mine to a shoe store. My heart was weighing as much as cord-wood, and so I forgot the wire until I was having the shoes fitted. When I opened it and read that *Jonah's Gourd Vine* was accepted and that Lippincott was offering me $200 advance, I tore out of that place with one old shoe and one new one on and ran to the Western Union office. Lippincott had asked for an answer by wire and they got it! Terms accepted. I never expect to have a greater thrill than that wire gave me. You know the feeling when you found your first pubic hair. Greater than that. When Producer Arthur Hornblow took me to lunch at Lucey's and hired me at Paramount, it was nice—very nice. I was most elated. But I had had five books accepted then, been a Guggenheim fellow twice, spoken at three book fairs with all the literary greats of America and some from abroad, and so I was a little more used to things. So you see why Bertram Lippincott is *Colonel* Bert to me. When the Negroes in the south name a white man a colonel, it means CLASS. Something like a monarch, only bigger and better. And when the colored population in the south confer a title, the white people recognize it because the Negroes are never wrong. They may flatter an ordinary bossman by calling him "Cap'n" but when they say "Colonel," "General," and "Governor" they are recognizing something internal. It is there, and it is accepted because it can be seen.

I wrote *Their Eyes Were Watching God* in Haiti. It was dammed up in me, and I wrote it under internal pressure in seven weeks. I wish that I could write it again. In fact, I regret all of my books. It is one of the tragedies of life that one cannot have all the wisdom one is ever to possess in the beginning. Perhaps, it is just as well to be rash and foolish for a while. If writers were too wise, perhaps no books would get written at all. It might be better to ask yourself "Why?" afterwards than before. Anyway, the force from somewhere in Space which commands you to write in the first place, gives you no choice. You take up the pen when you are told and write what is commanded. There is no agony like bearing an untold story inside you. You have all heard of the Spartan youth with the fox under his cloak.

Dust Tracks on a Road is being written in California where I did not expect to be at this time.

I did not come out here to California to write about the state. I did not come to get into the movies. I came because my good friend, Katharane Edson Mershon, invited me out here to rest and have a good time. However, I have written a book here, and gone to work in the movies. This surprises me because I did not think that I would live long enough to do anything out here but die. Friend Katharane Mershon is a mountain goat while I am a lowland turtle. I want to rock along on level ground. She can't look at a mountain without leaping on it. I think she is ashamed if she ever catches both of her feet on the same level. She cries "Excelsior!" in her sleep. Jack, her husband, told me that the reason he has that sort of smoothed-off look was because she dragged him up a mountain the next day after they got married and he has never been able to get his right shape back again. Well, 1941 was a hard year for me, too. She showed me California. Before it was over, I felt like I had spent two months walking a cross-cut saw. The minute I get to be governor of California, I mean to get me an over-sized plane and a spirit-level and fix this state so it can be looked at without rearing back. EPIC nothing! LEVEL! Level California! And I do mean L E V E L !!!!

My People! My People!

"My people! My people!" From the earliest rocking of my cradle days, I have heard this cry go up from Negro lips. It is forced outward by pit, scorn and hopeless resignation. It is called forth by the observations of one class of Negro on the doings of another branch of the brother in black. For instance, well-mannered Negroes groan out like that when they board a train or a bus and find other Negroes on there with their shoes off, stuffing themselves with fried fish, bananas and peanuts, and throwing the garbage on the floor. Maybe they are not only eating and drinking. The offenders may be "loud-talking" the place, and holding back nothing of their private lives, in a voice that embraces the entire coach. The well-dressed Negro shrinks back in his seat at that, shakes his head and sighs, "My people! My people!"

Now, the well-mannered Negro is embarrassed by the crude behavior of the others. They are not friends, and have never seen each other before. So why should he or she be embarrassed? It is like this: The well-bred Negro has looked around and seen America with his eyes. He or she has set himself to measure up to what he thinks of as the white standard of living. He is conscious of the fact that the Negro in America needs more respect if he expects to get any acceptance at all. Therefore, after straining every nerve to get an education, maintain an attractive home, dress decently, and otherwise conform, he is dismayed at the sight of other Negroes tearing down what he is trying to build up. It is said every day, "And that good-for-nothing, trashy Negro is the one the white people judge us all by. They think we're all just alike. My people! My people!" . . .

Poetry Is Practical

LANGSTON HUGHES

My poems sent me to college.

Born in Joplin, Missouri, James Mercer Langston Hughes (1902–1967) was best known as a prominent poet and writer of short stories, novels, plays, nonfiction, and books for children. During the Harlem Renaissance of the 1920s, his popular character, Jesse B. Semple, commonly known as Simple, symbolized with humor and down-home wisdom the everyday Black man on the opinions and topics of the day. The winner of numerous poetry and writing awards, Hughes served as a columnist for the *Chicago Defender* for twenty years.

Widely traveled, Hughes wrote about his journeys in his two autobiographies, *The Big Sea* and *I Wonder as I Wander*. His father tried to encourage him to remove himself from American racism by relocating to Mexico as he had done. Saying he liked being around Negroes, the younger Hughes stayed in the States and held a variety of jobs in Washington, DC, including one with historian Carter G. Woodson, the "father" of Black History Month. This excerpt from *The Big Sea* tells us how Hughes longed to go to college, and how he wrote his way there.

Working in the steam of the wet wash laundry that winter, I caught a bad cold, stayed home from work a week—and found my job gone when I went back. So I went to work for a colored newspaper. But I only made eighty cents in two weeks, so I quit the newspaper game. Then an old school friend of my mother's, Amanda Grey Hilyer, who once owned a drug store, spoke to Dr. Carter G. Woodson about me, and Dr. Woodson gave me a job in the offices of the Association for the Study of Negro Life and History as his personal assistant.

My new job paid several dollars more a week than the wet wash laundry. It was what they call in Washington "a position." But it was much harder work than the laundry.

I had to go to work early and start the furnace in the morning, dust, open the office, and see that the stenographers came in on time. Then I had to sort the mail, notify Dr. Woodson of callers, wrap and post all book orders, keep the office routine going, read proof, check address lists, help on the typing, fold and seal letters, run errands, lock up, clean the office in the evening—and then come back and bank the furnace every night at nine!

At that time Dr. Woodson was working on his compilation, *Thirty Thousand Free Negro Heads of Families*. My job was to put the thirty thousand in alphabetical order from *Ab, Abner*, on down to *Zu, Zucker*, or whatever the last name might be—from the first letter of each name alphabetically through to the last letter of each name, in absolute order. They were typed on thirty thousand slips of paper. The job took weeks. Then checking the proofs took weeks more. It was like arranging a telephone book, and only myself to do it—along with my other work.

Although I realized what a fine contribution Dr. Woodson was making to the Negro people and to America, publishing his histories, his studies, and his *Journal of Negro History*, I personally did not like the work I had to do. Besides, it hurt my eyes. So when I got through the proofs, I decided I didn't care to have "a position" any longer, I preferred a job, so I went to work at the Wardman Park Hotel as a bus boy, where meals were thrown in and it was less hard on the sight, although the pay was not quite the same and there was no dignity attached to bus boy work in the eyes of upper class Washingtonians, who kept insisting that a colored poet should be a credit to his race.

But I am glad I went to work at the Wardman Park Hotel, because there I met Vachel Lindsay. Diplomats and cabinet members in the dining room did not excite me much, but I was thrilled the day Vachel Lindsay came. I knew him, because I'd seen his picture in the papers that morning. He was to give a reading of his poems in the little theater of the hotel that night. I wanted very much to hear him read his poems, but I knew they did not admit colored people to the auditorium.

That afternoon I wrote out three of my poems, "Jazzonia," "Negro Dancers," and "The Weary Blues," on some pieces of paper and put them in the pocket of my white bus boy's coat. In the evening when Mr. Lindsay came down to dinner, quickly I laid them beside his plate and went away, afraid to say anything to so famous a poet, except to tell him I liked his poems and that these were poems of mine. I looked back once and saw Mr. Lindsay reading the poems, as I picked up a tray of dirty dishes from a side table and started for the dumb-waiter.

The next morning on the way to work, as usual I bought a paper—and there I read that Vachel Lindsay had discovered a Negro bus boy poet! At the hotel the reporters were already waiting for me. They interviewed me. And they took my picture, holding up a tray of dirty dishes in the middle of the dining room. The picture, copyrighted by Underwood and Underwood, appeared in lots of newspapers throughout the country. It was my first publicity break.

Mr. Lindsay had gone, but he left a package for me at the desk, a set of Amy Lowell's *John Keats*, with this note written on the fly leaves:

December 6, 1925
Wardman Park Hotel,
Washington, D.C.

My dear Langston Hughes:

The "New Poetry" movement has been going on in America
since 1912. Two members of that army have died—Joyce
Kilmer in the war, and Amy Lowell very recently. Already
one hundred distinguished books of verse or criticism have
been written and hundreds of poems set going.

Eleven of the distinguished books are by Amy Lowell—
and are listed in the front of this one. Please read the books
and ignore the newspapers. I should say "Tendencies in
Modern American Poetry" by Miss Lowell is a good book to
start on. You may know all of this better than I do.

Miss Lowell has re-written the story of Keats from the
standpoint of the "New Poetry." I hope you care to go
into the whole movement for study from Edwin Arlington
Robinson to Alfred Kreymborg's "Troubadour."

Do not let any lionizers stampede you. Hide and write
and study and think. I know what factions do. Beware of
them. I know what flatterers do. Beware of them. I know
what lionizers do. Beware of them.

Good wishes to you indeed,
(Signed) Nicholas Vachel Lindsay

Permanent address:
Room 1129
Davenport Hotel
Spokane, Washington

This note was written in ink in great, flowing, generous hand-
writing, spread over six pages—all the pages there were before the

book proper began. A few days later Mr. Lindsay and his wife came back to the hotel, passing through Washington on the way to another engagement, and I had a short, encouraging talk with him. He was a great, kind man. And he is one of the people I remember with pleasure and gratitude out of my bewildered days in Washington.

Poetry Is Practical

The widespread publicity resulting from the Vachel Lindsay incident was certainly good for my poetic career, but it was not good for my job, because from then on, very often the head waiter would call me to come and stand before some table whose curious guests wished to see what a Negro bus boy poet looked like. I felt self-conscious and embarrassed, so when pay day came, I quit.

I went home, went to bed, and stayed in bed ten days. I was not sick, just tired of working. My mother said she was tired of working, too, and I could either get up from there and go back to work, or I would not eat! But I was really tired, so I stayed right on in bed and rested and read—and got hungry. My mother refused to feed me on the food she prepared for my little brother when she got home from work. And I didn't blame her, if she didn't want to feed me.

One day a young Howard student named Edward Lovette came by the house to show me something that he had written. I had never met him before, but I told him I was hungry, so he invited me to come with him to a restaurant and have lunch. Every day for several days the same student came by and bought me a meal, although he didn't have much money. I will never forget him, because I needed those meals.

While in Washington I won my first poetry prize. *Opportunity* magazine, the official publication of the National Urban League, held its first literary contest. In succeeding years, two others were held with funds given by Casper Holstein, a wealthy West Indian numbers banker who did good things with his money, such as educating boys and girls at colleges in the South, building decent apartment houses in Harlem, and backing literary contests to encourage colored writers. Mr. Holstein, no doubt, would have been snubbed in polite Washington society, Negro or white, but there he was doing decent and helpful things that it hadn't occurred to lots of others to do. Certainly he was a great help to poor poets.

I sent several poems to the first contest. And then, as an afterthought, I sent "The Weary Blues," the poem I had written three winters before up the Hudson and whose ending I had never been able to get quite right. But I thought perhaps it was as right now as it would ever be. It was a poem about a working man who sang the blues all night and then went to bed and slept like a rock. That was all. And it included the first blues verse I'd ever heard way back in Lawrence, Kansas, when I was a kid.

> *I got de weary blues*
> *And I can't be satisfied.*
> *Got de weary blues*
> *And can't be satisfied.*
> *I ain't happy no mo'*
> *And I wish that I had died.*

That was my lucky poem—because it won the first prize.

The prizes were to be awarded at a banquet in New York. The poetry prize was forty dollars. I spent it going after it. But it was a good banquet, where I met Clement Wood and again saw James Weldon Johnson, who, with Witter Bynner and John Farrar, were the poetry judges. Also I met Zora Neale Hurston and Eric Walrond, who were among the prize winners in other fields.

James Weldon Johnson read my poem aloud to the assemblage in awarding me the prize. And after the banquet was over, Carl Van Vechten came up to congratulate me. It was the first time I had seen him since being introduced to him at the N.A.A.C.P. benefit party in Harlem, but he remembered me, and asked if I had enough poems by now to make a book. I told him I thought I had, so he asked me to send them to him to read.

When I got back to Washington, I promptly sent Mr. Van Vechten my poems. He wrote saying that he liked them, and asked permission to submit my manuscript to his publishers, Alfred A. Knopf. And shortly there came a letter from Blanche Knopf, saying my poems were to be accepted for publication. I called the book *The Weary Blues*.

When I was tired of resting after the Wardman Park, I got a job at a fish and oyster house in downtown Washington. (I always liked jobs in places where you eat.) I wore a tall white cap like Bruce's, and I stood behind a counter twelve hours a day, making oyster stews and oyster cocktails to order. My first week there I ate so many oysters myself that I broke out all over in an oyster rash. Now that I had won a prize, I began to meet all the other young colored poets in Washington. Georgia Douglas Johnson, a charming woman poet, who had two sons in college, turned her house into a salon for us on Saturday nights. Marietta Bonner, Dutton Ferguson, Esther Popel, Richard Bruce Nugent, Mae Miller, Lewis Alexander, John P. Davis, Willis Richardson, Hallie Queen, and Clarissa Scott used to come there to eat Mrs. Johnson's cake and drink her wine and talk poetry and books and plays. Sometimes Alain Locke would drop in, too. And that year I met Angelina Grimke.

My two years in Washington were unhappy years, except for poetry and the friends I made through poetry. I wrote many poems. I always put them away new for several weeks in a bottom drawer. Then I would take them out and re-read them. If they seemed bad, I would throw them away. They would all seem good when I wrote them and, usually, bad when I would look at them again. So most of them were thrown away.

The blues poems I would often make up in my head and sing on the way to work. (Except that I could never carry a tune. But when I sing to myself, I think I am singing.) One evening, I was crossing Rock Creek Bridge, singing a blues I was trying to get right before I put it down on paper. A man passing on the opposite side of the bridge stopped, looked at me, then turned around and cut across the roadway.

He said: "Son, what's the matter? Are you ill?"

"No," I said. "Just singing."

"I thought you were groaning," he commented. "Sorry!" And went his way.

So after that I never sang my verses aloud in the street any more.

It seems that Carl Van Vechten had spoken to Margaret Case about my work, so *Vanity Fair* bought some of my poems, the first I sold. And paid well for them. Next I believe the *New Republic* and the *Bookman* bought my work, sending checks that were small, but encouraging. I was particularly glad that Ridgeley Torrence at the *New Republic* had liked my poems.

Then I won another literary prize, one of the Amy Spingarn prizes offered by the *Crisis*. In New York I met Mrs. Spingarn, and was invited to her home for tea. She lived then in West 73rd Street in a tall house with an elevator. I had never seen a private house with an elevator before, so I was much intrigued by it. Mrs. Spingarn had a studio at the top of the house, where she made some sketches of me that later developed into a portrait in oils. As she sketched, the maid brought tea and cinnamon toast, and Mrs. Spingarn recited Wordsworth and Shelley in a deep voice.

During that same trip to New York, Winold Reiss made a portrait of me in colored crayons, and at Eric Walrond's place in Harlem, I met a young Mexican artist named Miguel Covarrubias, who was fascinated by Harlem and made wonderful caricatures in rhythm of dancers and blues singers. About that time I met Aaron Douglas, too, and Augusta Savage, the sculptress, and Gwendolyn Bennett, who was both an artist and a poet. I began to form my first literary and artistic friendships.

In those days, Charles S. Johnson, writer, speaker, and social scientist, was the editor of *Opportunity*. Mr. Johnson, I believe, did more to encourage and develop Negro writers during the 1920's than anyone else in America. He wrote them sympathetic letters, pointing out the merits of their work. He brought them together to meet and know each other. He made the *Opportunity* contests sources of discovery and help.

Jessie Faucet at the *Crisis*, Charles Johnson at *Opportunity*, and Alain Locke in Washington, were the three people who midwifed the so-called New Negro literature into being. Kind and critical—but not too critical for the young—they nursed us along until our books were born. Countee Cullen, Zora Neale Hurston, Arna Bontemps, Rudolph Fisher, Wallace Thurman, Jean Toomer, Nella Larsen, all of us came along about the same time. Most of us are quite grown up now. Some are silent. Some are dead.

One day on a street car in Washington, I first met Waring Cuney. He had a *Chicago Defender*, oldest American Negro newspaper, in his hand, and my picture was in the *Defender* with the announcement of the forthcoming publication of *The Weary Blues*. Cuney looked from the picture to me, then asked if I were one and the same. I said yes. Then he said he wrote poetry, too. I said I'd like to see it, so later he brought some of his poems to show me.

Cuney was a student at Lincoln University, near Philadelphia. He told me it was a fine college, because you had plenty of time there to read and write. He said the tuition was cheaper than at Howard. So I sent for a catalogue of the college courses at Lincoln, since it seemed I would never be able to enter Howard, anyway.

One afternoon I had had tea with a woman in New York to whom I mentioned that I was trying to find a way to go back to college. I said I wanted to find out what makes the world the kind of world it is. She had one son in college herself, and so was very sympathetic. The next time I saw her, I told her about Lincoln. She listened and at Christmas, the Christmas of 1925, there came a letter from her, offering me a scholarship at Lincoln. It was the happiest holiday gift I've ever received. My poems had caused me to meet her. My poems—through the kindness of this woman who liked poetry—sent me to college. So at mid-year I entered Lincoln, and remained there until I received my degree.

The Business of the Writer

JAMES BALDWIN

I read just about everything I could get
my hands on—except the Bible, the only
book I was encouraged to read.

James Baldwin was born in 1924. At an early age at schools in New York
City, he held a passion for reading and showed a talent for writing. In the
1960s, his highly acclaimed novels and essays, articulating the issues
of race and humanity, made him an important voice of the civil rights
movement. He settled in Saint-Paul de Vence, France, where he died in
1987. Nobel Prize winner Toni Morrison, a friend of his, has said that
his passing left an intellectual void.

In these "Autobiographical Notes" from his classic book of essays,
Notes of a Native Son, which has been continuously in print since its
publication in 1955, Baldwin describes the unique dilemma of being a
"Negro writer expected to write about the Negro problem."

was born in Harlem thirty-one years ago. I began plotting novels at about the time I learned to read. The story of my childhood is the usual bleak fantasy, and we can dismiss it with the restrained observation that I certainly would not consider living it again. In those days my mother was given to the exasperating and mysterious habit of having babies. As they were born, I took them over with one hand and held a book with the other. The children probably suffered, though they have since been kind enough to deny it, and in this way I read *Uncle Tom's Cabin* and *A Tale of Two Cities* over and over and over again; in this way, in fact, I read just about everything I could get my hands on—except the Bible, probably because it was the only book I was encouraged to read. I must also confess that I wrote—a great deal—and my first professional triumph, in any case, the first effort of mine to be seen in print, occurred at the age of twelve or thereabouts, when a short story I had written about the Spanish revolution won some sort of prize in an extremely short-lived church newspaper. I remember the story was censored by the lady editor, though I don't remember why, and I was outraged.

Also wrote plays, and songs, for one of which I received a letter of congratulations from Mayor La Guardia, and poetry, about which the less said, the better. My mother was delighted by all these goings-on, but my father wasn't; he wanted me to be a preacher. When I was fourteen I became a preacher, and when I was seventeen I stopped. Very shortly thereafter I left home. For God knows how long I struggled with the world of commerce and industry—I guess they would say they struggled with *me*—and when I was about twenty-one I had enough done of a novel to get a Saxton Fellowship. When I was twenty-two the fellowship was over, the novel turned out to be unsalable, and I started waiting on tables in a Village restaurant and writing book reviews—mostly, as it turned out, about the Negro problem, concerning which the color of my skin made me automatically an expert. Did another book, in company with photographer Theodore Pelatowski, about the store-front churches in Harlem. This book met exactly the same fate as my first—fellow-ship, but no sale. (It was a Rosenwald Fellowship.) By the time I was twenty-four I had decided to stop reviewing books about the Negro problem—which by this time, was only slightly less horrible in print than it was in life—and I packed my bags and went to France, where I finished, God knows how, *Go Tell It on the Mountain*.

Any writer, I suppose, feels that the world into which he was born is nothing less than a conspiracy against the cultivation of his talent—which attitude certainly has a great deal to support it. On the other hand, it is only because the world looks on his talent with such a frightening indifference that the artist is compelled to make his talent important. So that any writer, looking back over even so short a span of time as I am here forced to assess, finds that the things which hurt him and the things which helped him cannot be divorced from each other; he could be helped in a certain way only because he was hurt in a certain way; and his help is simply to be enabled to move from one conundrum to the next—one is tempted to say that he moves from one disaster to the next. When one begins looking for influences one finds them by the score. I haven't thought much about my own, not enough anyway; I hazard that the King James Bible, the rhetoric of the store-front church, something ironic and violent and perpetually understated in Negro speech—and something of Dickens' love for bravura—have something to do with me today; but I wouldn't stake my life on it. Likewise, innumerable people have helped me in many ways; but finally, I suppose, the most difficult (and most rewarding) thing in my life has been the fact that I was born a Negro and was forced, therefore, to effect some kind of truce with this reality. (Truce, by the way, is the best one can hope for.)

One of the difficulties about being a Negro writer (and this is not special pleading, since I don't mean to suggest that he has it worse than anybody else) is that the Negro problem is written about so widely. The bookshelves groan under the weight of information, and everyone therefore considers himself informed. And this information, furthermore, operates usually (generally, popularly) to

reinforce traditional attitudes. Of traditional attitudes there are only
two—For or Against—and I, personally, find it difficult to say which
attitude has caused me the most pain. I am speaking as a writer;
from a social point of view I am perfectly aware that the change
from ill-will to good-will, however motivated, however imperfect,
however expressed, is better than no change at all.

But it is part of the business of the writer—as I see it—to examine attitudes, to go beneath the surface, to tap the source. From
this point of view the Negro problem is nearly inaccessible. It is not
only written about so widely; it is written about so badly. It is quite
possible to say that the price a Negro pays for becoming articulate is
to find himself, at length, with nothing to be articulate about. ("You
taught me language," says Caliban to Prospero, "and my profit on't
is I know how to curse.") Consider: the tremendous social activity
that this problem generates imposes on whites and Negroes alike
the necessity of looking forward, of working to bring about a better
day. This is fine, it keeps the waters troubled; it is all, indeed, that
has made possible to the Negro's progress. Nevertheless, social affairs are not generally speaking the writer's prime concern, whether
they ought to be or not; it is absolutely necessary that he establish
between himself and these affairs a distance which will allow, at
least, for clarity, so that before he can look forward in any meaningful sense, he must first be allowed to take a long look back. In
the context of the Negro problem neither whites nor blacks, for
excellent reasons of their own, have the faintest desire to look back;
but I think that the past is all that makes the present coherent, and
further, that the past will remain horrible for exactly as long as we
refuse to assess it honestly.

I know, in any case, that the most crucial time in my own development came when I was forced to recognize that I was a kind of
bastard of the West; when I followed the line of my past I did not
find myself in Europe but in Africa. And this meant that in some
subtle way, in a really profound way, I brought to Shakespeare, Bach,
Rembrandt, to the stones of Paris, to the cathedral of Chartres, and
to the Empire State Building, a special attitude. These were not re-

ally my creations, they did not contain my history; I might search in them in vain forever for any reflection of myself. I was an interloper; this was not my heritage. At the same time I had no other heritage which I could possibly hope to use—I had certainly been unfitted for the jungle or the tribe. I would have to appropriate these white centuries, I would have to make them mine—I would have to accept my special attitude, my special place in this scheme—otherwise I would have no place in *any* scheme. What was the most difficult was the fact that I was forced to admit something I had always hidden from myself, which the American Negro has had to hide from himself as the price of his public progress; that I hated and feared white people. This did not mean that I loved black people; on the contrary, I despised them, possibly because they failed to produce Rembrandt. In effect, I hated and feared the world. And this meant, not only that I thus gave the world an altogether murderous power over me, but also that in such a self-destroying limbo I could never hope to write.

One writes out of one thing only—one's own experience. Everything depends on how relentlessly one forces from this experience the last drop, sweet or bitter, it can possibly give. This is the only real concern of the artist, to recreate out of the disorder of life that order which is art. The difficulty then, for me, of being a Negro writer was the fact that I was, in effect, prohibited from examining my own experience too closely by the tremendous demands and the very real dangers of my social situation.

I don't think the dilemma outlined above is uncommon. I do think, since writers work in the disastrously explicit medium of language, that it goes a little way towards explaining why, out of the enormous resources of Negro speech and life, and despite the example of Negro music, prose written by Negroes has been generally speaking so pallid and so harsh. I have not written about being a Negro at such length because I expect that to be my only subject, but only because it was the gate I had to unlock before I could hope to write about anything else. I don't think that the Negro problem in America can be even discussed coherently without bearing in mind its context; its context being the history, traditions, customs, the moral assumptions and preoccupations of the country; in short, the general social fabric. Appearance to the contrary, no one in America escapes its effects and everyone in America bears some responsibility for it. I believe this the more firmly because it is the overwhelming tendency to speak of this problem as though it were a thing apart. But in the work of Faulkner, in the general attitude and certain specific passages in Robert Penn Warren, and, most significantly, the advent of Ralph Ellison, one sees the beginnings—at least—of a more genuinely penetrating search. Mr. Ellison, by the way, is the first Negro novelist I have ever read to utilize in language, and brilliantly, some of the ambiguity and irony of Negro life.

About my interests: I don't know if I have any, unless the morbid desire to own a sixteen-millimeter camera and make experimental movies can be so classified. Otherwise, I love to eat and drink—it's my melancholy conviction that I've scarcely ever had enough to eat (this is because it's *impossible* to eat enough if you're worried about the next meal)—and I love to argue with people who do not disagree with me too profoundly, and I love to laugh. I do *not* like bohemia, or bohemians, I do not like people whose principal aim is pleasure, and I do not like people who are *earnest* about anything. I don't like people who like me because I'm a Negro; neither do I like people who find in the same accident grounds for contempt. I love America more than any other country in the world, and, exactly for this reason, I insist on the right to criticize her perpetually. I think all theories are suspect, that the finest principles may have to be modified, or may even be pulverized by the demands of life, and that one must find, therefore, one's own moral center and move through the world hoping that this center will guide one aright. I consider that I have many responsibilities, but none greater than this: to last, as Hemingway says, and get my work done.

I want to be an honest man and a good writer.

Turning Point

MALCOLM X

I was one of the school's top students—
but all he could see for me was the
kind of future "in your place."

Malcolm X (1925–1965) was a charismatic, inspirational, and prominent Black nationalist. Serving as a spokesperson for the Nation of Islam
for more than a decade, in speeches, public appearances, and media
interviews, he articulated the deep-seated frustrations and opinions of
African Americans in dealing with society's racism. Affirming self-worth
and the ability for self-determination if allowed equal opportunity, Malcolm X became one of the most quoted and admired leaders among
Black people. He also gained international acclaim, as evidenced in his
invitations to speak, such as in debate at the Oxford Union Society in
1964, which was televised on the BBC.

　　Malcolm X was acutely aware of the power of words. Born with the
last name Little, when he became a member of the Nation of Islam in
1952, as was the custom of the racially proud and religious organiza-
tion, he replaced it with an "X" as a symbol of African Americans' denied ancestral African names and the forced use of last names of slave
masters (that have been passed down generationally to this day). After
his religious pilgrimage to Mecca, in which he felt he had encountered
brotherhood with Whites for the first time, he became a Sunni Muslim
and asserted a new name again, in the custom of those who make hajj,
to El-Hajj Malik El-Shabazz.

In the months before his assassination, he collaborated with writer Alex Haley on his autobiography. In this excerpt, he shares the story of his early education, those impressionable years of learning in which a teacher's words can motivate a student—or reinforce society's low expectations that will affect one's life forever.

That summer of 1940, in Lansing, I caught the Greyhound bus for Boston with my cardboard suitcase, and wearing my green suit. If someone had hung a sign, "HICK," around my neck, I couldn't have looked much more obvious. They didn't have the turnpikes then; the bus stopped at what seemed every corner and cowpatch. From my seat in—you guessed it—the back of the bus, I gawked out of the window at white man's America rolling past for what seemed a month, but must have been only a day and a half.

When we finally arrived, Ella met me at the terminal and took me home. The house was on Waumbeck Street in the Sugar Hill section of Roxbury, the Harlem of Boston. I met Ella's second husband, Frank, who was now a soldier; and her brother Earl, the singer who called himself Jimmy Carleton; and Mary, who was very different from her older sister. It's funny how I seemed to think of Mary as Ella's sister, instead of her being, just as Ella is, my own half-sister. It's probably because Ella and I always were much closer as basic types; we're dominant people, and Mary has always been mild and quiet, almost shy.

Ella was busily involved in dozens of things. She belonged to I don't know how many different clubs; she was a leading light of local so-called "black society." I saw and met a hundred black people there whose big-city talk and ways left my mouth hanging open.

I couldn't have feigned indifference if I had tried to. People talked casually about Chicago, Detroit, New York. I didn't know the world contained as many Negroes as I saw thronging downtown Roxbury at night, especially on Saturdays. Neon lights, nightclubs, poolhalls, bars, the cars they drove! Restaurants made the streets smell—rich, greasy, down-home black cooking! Jukeboxes blared to Erskine Hawkins, Duke Ellington, Cootie Williams, dozens of others. If somebody had told me then that some day I'd know them all personally, I'd have found it hard to believe. The biggest bands, like these, played at the Roseland State Ballroom, on Boston's Massachusetts Avenue—one night for Negroes, the next night for whites.

I saw for the first time occasional black-white couples strolling around arm in arm. And on Sundays, when Ella, Mary, or somebody took me to church, I saw churches for black people such as I had never seen. They were many times finer than the white church I had attended back in Mason, Michigan. There, the white people just sat and worshiped with words; but the Boston Negroes, like all other Negroes I had ever seen at church, threw their souls and bodies wholly into worship.

Two or three times, I wrote letters to Wilfred intended for everybody back in Lansing. I said I'd try to describe it when I got back. But I found I couldn't.

My restlessness with Mason—and for the first time in my life a restlessness with being around white people—began as soon as I got back home and entered eighth grade.

I continued to think constantly about all that I had seen in Boston, and about the way I had felt there. I know now that it was the sense of being a real part of a mass of my own kind, for the first time.

The white people—classmates, the Swerlins, the people at the restaurant where I worked—noticed the change. They said, "You're acting so strange. You don't seem like yourself, Malcolm. What's the matter?"

I kept close to the top of the class, though. The top-most scholastic standing, I remember, kept shifting between me, a girl named Audrey Slaugh, and a boy named Jimmy Cotton.

It went on that way, as I became increasingly restless and disturbed through the first semester. And then one day, just about when those of us who had passed were about to move up to 8-A, from which we would enter high school the next year, something happened which was to become the first major turning point of my life.

Somehow, I happened to be alone in the classroom with Mr. Ostrowski, my English teacher. He was a tall, rather reddish white man and he had a thick mustache. I had gotten some of my best marks under him, and he had always made me feel that he liked me. He was, as I have mentioned, a natural-born "advisor," about what you ought to read, to do, or think—about any and everything. We used to make unkind jokes about him: why was he teaching in Mason instead of somewhere else, getting for himself some of the "success in life" that he kept telling us how to get?

I know that he probably meant well in what he happened to advise me that day. I doubt that he meant any harm. It was just in his nature as an American white man. I was one of his top students, one of the school's top students—but all he could see for me was the kind of future "in your place" that almost all white people see for black people.

He told me, "Malcolm, you ought to be thinking about a career. Have you been giving it thought?"

The truth is, I hadn't. I never have figured out why I told him, "Well, yes, sir, I've been thinking I'd like to be a lawyer." Lansing certainly had no Negro lawyers—or doctors either—in those days, to hold up an image I might have aspired to. All I really knew for certain was that a lawyer didn't wash dishes, as I was doing.

Mr. Ostrowski looked surprised, I remember, and leaned back in his chair and clasped his hands behind his head. He kind of half-smiled and said, "Malcolm, one of life's first needs is for us to be realistic. Don't misunderstand me, now. We all here like you, you know that. But you've got to be realistic about being a nigger. A lawyer—that's no realistic goal for a nigger. You need to think about something you *can* be. You're good with your hands—making things. Everybody admires your carpentry shop work. Why don't you plan on carpentry? People like you as a person—you'd get all kinds of work."

The more I thought afterwards about what he said, the more uneasy it made me. It just kept treading around in my mind.

What made it really begin to disturb me was Mr. Ostrowski's advice to others in my class—all of them white. Most of them had told him they were planning to become farmers. But those who wanted to strike out on their own, to try something new, he had encouraged. Some, mostly girls, wanted to be teachers. A few wanted other professions, such as one boy who wanted to become a county agent; another, a veterinarian; and one girl wanted to be a nurse. They all reported that Mr. Ostrowski had encouraged what they had wanted. Yet nearly none of them had earned marks equal to mine.

It was a surprising thing that I had never thought of it that way before, but I realized that whatever I wasn't, I *was* smarter than nearly all of those white kids. But apparently, I was still not intelligent enough, in their eyes, to become whatever *I* wanted to be.

It was then that I began to change—inside.

I drew away from white people. I came to class, and I answered when called upon. It became a physical strain simply to sit in Mr. Ostrowski's class.

Where "nigger" had slipped off my back before, wherever I heard it now, I stopped and looked at whoever said it. And they looked surprised that I did.

I quit hearing so much "nigger" and "What's wrong?"—which was the way I wanted it. Nobody, including the teachers, could decide what had come over me. I knew I was being discussed.

In a few more weeks, it was that way, too, at the restaurant where I worked washing dishes, and at the Swerlins'.

One day soon after, Mrs. Swerlin called me into the living room, and there was the state man, Maynard Allen. I knew from their faces that something was about to happen. She told me that none of them could understand why—after I had done so well in school, and on my job, and living with them, and after everyone in Mason had come to like me—I had lately begun to make them all feel that I wasn't happy there anymore.

She said she felt there was no need for me to stay at the detention home any longer, and that arrangements had been made for me to go and live with the Lyons family, who liked me so much.

She stood up and put out her hand. "I guess I've asked you a hundred times, Malcolm—do you want to tell me what's wrong?"

I shook her hand, and said, "Nothing, Mrs. Swerlin." Then I went and got my things, and came back down. At the living room door I saw her wiping her eyes. I felt very bad. I thanked her and went out in front to Mr. Allen, who took me over to the Lyons'.

Mr. and Mrs. Lyons, and their children, during the two months I lived with them—while finishing eighth grade—also tried to get me to tell them what was wrong. But somehow I couldn't tell them, either.

I went every Saturday to see my brothers and sisters in Lansing, and almost every other day I wrote to Ella in Boston. Not saying why, I told Ella that I wanted to come there and live.

I don't know how she did it, but she arranged for official custody of me to be transferred from Michigan to Massachusetts, and the very week I finished the eighth grade, I again boarded the Greyhound bus for Boston.

I've thought about that time a lot since then. No physical move in my life has been more pivotal or profound in its repercussions.

If I had stayed on in Michigan, I would probably have married one of those Negro girls I knew and liked in Lansing. I might have become one of those state capitol building shoeshine boys, or a Lansing Country Club waiter, or gotten one of the other menial jobs which, in those days, among Lansing Negroes, would have been considered "successful"—or even become a carpenter.

Whatever I have done since then, I have driven myself to become a success at it. I've often thought that if Mr. Ostrowski had encouraged me to become a lawyer, I would today probably be among some city's professional black bourgeoisie, sipping cocktails and palming myself off as a community spokesman for and leader of the suffering black masses, while my primary concern would be to grab a few more crumbs from the groaning board of the two-faced whites with whom they're begging to "integrate."

All praise is due to Allah that I went to Boston when I did. If I hadn't, I'd probably still be a brainwashed black Christian.

Lessons in Living

MAYA ANGELOU

Mrs. Flowers taught me that I must always be intolerant
of ignorance but understanding of illiteracy.

Maya Angelou (1928–2014), poet, dancer, playwright, essayist, and author of a groundbreaking series of memoirs, was a cultural and political
activist who worked with both Martin Luther King Jr. and Malcolm X in
the civil rights movement. In 1993, she was invited by President Bill
Clinton to deliver a poetry recitation at his inauguration, the first poet
to do so since Robert Frost recited at President John F. Kennedy's 1961
swearing-in. The poem she wrote was "On the Pulse of Morning." Also
known as "the Black woman's poet laureate," Angelou published more
than a dozen poetry collections. Two of Angelou's most popular and
oft-recited poems are "Still I Rise" and "Phenomenal Woman."

Given her inspirational oratorical fame, it may be little known that as
a child she refused to speak for several years. In this story from *I Know
Why the Caged Bird Sings*, the first nonfiction bestseller by an African
American woman and the beginning memoir in her series of autobiographies (among her thirty-six books), Angelou tells us how books gave her
back her voice.

had to stop talking.

I discovered that to achieve perfect personal silence all I had to do was to attach myself leechlike to sound. I began to listen to everything. I probably hoped that after I had heard all the sounds, really heard them and packed them down, deep in my ears, the world would be quiet around me. I walked into rooms where people were laughing, their voices hitting the walls like stones, and I simply stood still—in the midst of the riot of sound. After a minute or two, silence would rush into the room from its hiding place because I had eaten up all the sounds.

In the first weeks my family accepted my behavior as a post-rape, post-hospital affliction. (Neither the term nor the experience was mentioned in Grandmother's house, where Bailey and I were again staying.) They understood that I could talk to Bailey, but to no one else.

Then came the last visit from the visiting nurse, and the doctor said I was healed. That meant that I should be back on the sidewalks playing handball or enjoying the games I had been given when I was sick. When I refused to be the child they knew and accepted me to be, I was called impudent and my muteness sullenness.

For a while I was punished for being so uppity that I wouldn't speak; and then came the thrashings, given by any relative who felt himself offended.

We were on the train going back to Stamps, and this time it was I who had to console Bailey. He cried his heart out down the aisles of the coach, and pressed his little-boy body against the window pane looking for a last glimpse of his Mother Dear.

I have never known if Momma sent for us, or if the St. Louis family just got fed up with my grim presence. There is nothing more appalling than a constantly morose child.

I cared less about the trip than about the fact that Bailey was unhappy, and had no more thought of our destination than if I had simply been heading for the toilet.

The barrenness of Stamps was exactly what I wanted, without will or consciousness. After St. Louis, with its noise and activity, its trucks and buses, and loud family gatherings, I welcomed the obscure lanes and lonely bungalows set back deep in dirt yards.

The resignation of its inhabitants encouraged me to relax. They showed me a contentment based on the belief that nothing more was coming to them, although a great deal more was due. Their decision to be satisfied with life's inequities was a lesson for me. Entering Stamps, I had the feeling that I was stepping over the border lines of the map and would fall, without fear, right off the end of the world. Nothing more could happen, for in Stamps nothing happened.

Into this cocoon I crept.

For an indeterminate time, nothing was demanded of me or of Bailey. We were, after all, Mrs. Henderson's California grandchildren, and had been away on a glamorous trip way up North to the fabulous St. Louis. Our father had come the year before, driving a big, shiny automobile and speaking the King's English with a big city accent, so all we had to do was lie quiet for months and rake in the profits of our adventures.

Farmers and maids, cooks and handymen, carpenters and all the children in town, made regular pilgrimages to the Store. "Just to see the travelers."

They stood around like cutout cardboard figures and asked, "Well, how is it up North?"

"See any of them big buildings?"

"Ever ride in one of them elevators?"

"Was you scared?"

"Whitefolks any different, like they say?"

Bailey took it upon himself to answer every question, and from a corner of his lively imagination wove a tapestry of entertainment for them that I was sure was as foreign to him as it was to me.

He, as usual, spoke precisely. "They have, in the North, buildings so high that for months, in the winter, you can't see the top floors."

"Tell the truth."

"They've got watermelons twice the size of a cow's head and sweeter than syrup." I distinctly remember his intent face and the fascinated faces of his listeners. "And if you can count the watermelon's seeds, before it's cut open, you can win five zillion dollars and a new car."

Momma, knowing Bailey, warned, "Now Ju, be careful you don't slip up on a not true." (Nice people didn't say "lie.")

"Everybody wears new clothes and have inside toilets. If you fall down in one of them, you get flushed away into the Mississippi River. Some people have iceboxes, only the proper name is Cold Spot or Frigidaire. The snow is so deep you can get buried right outside your door and people won't find you for a year. We made ice cream out of the snow." That was the only fact that I could have supported. During the winter, we had collected a bowl of snow and poured Pet milk over it, and sprinkled it with sugar and called it ice cream.

Momma beamed and Uncle Willie was proud when Bailey regaled the customers with our exploits. We were drawing cards for the Store and objects of the town's adoration. Our journey to magical places alone was a spot of color on the town's drab canvas, and our return made us even more the most enviable of people.

High spots in Stamps were usually negative: droughts, floods, lynchings and deaths.

Bailey played on the country folks' need for diversion. Just after our return he had taken to sarcasm, picked it up as one might pick up a stone, and put it snufflike under his lip. The double entendres, the two-pronged sentences, slid over his tongue to dart rapier-like into anything that happened to be in the way. Our customers, though, generally were so straight thinking and speaking that they were never hurt by his attacks. They didn't comprehend them.

"Bailey Junior sound just like Big Bailey. Got a silver tongue. Just like his daddy."

"I hear tell they don't pick cotton up there. How the people live then?"

Bailey said that the cotton up North was so tall, if ordinary people tried to pick it they'd have to get up on ladders, so the cotton farmers had their cotton picked by machines.

For a while I was the only recipient of Bailey's kindness. It was not that he pitied me but that he felt we were in the same boat for different reasons and that I could understand his frustration just as he could countenance my withdrawal. . . .

People, except Momma and Uncle Willie, accepted my unwillingness to talk as a natural outgrowth of a reluctant return to the South. And an indication that I was pining for the high times we had had in the big city. Then, too, I was well known for being "tender-hearted." Southern Negroes used that term to mean sensitive and tended to look upon a person with that affliction as being a little sick or in delicate health. So I was not so much forgiven as I was understood.

———

For nearly a year, I sopped around the house, the Store, the school and the church, like an old biscuit, dirty and inedible. Then I met, or rather got to know, the lady who threw me my first life line.

Mrs. Bertha Flowers was the aristocrat of Black Stamps. She had the grace of control to appear warm in the coolest weather, and on the Arkansas summer days it seemed she had a private breeze which swirled around, cooling her. She was thin without the taut look of wry people, and her printed voile dresses and flowered hats were as right for her as denim overalls for a farmer. She was our side's answer to the richest white woman in town.

Her skin was a rich black that would have peeled like a plum if snagged, but then no one would have thought of getting close enough to Mrs. Flowers to ruffle her dress, let alone snag her skin. She didn't encourage familiarity. She wore gloves too.

I don't think I ever saw Mrs. Flowers laugh, but she smiled often. A slow widening of her thin black lips to show even, small white teeth, then the slow effortless closing. When she chose to smile on me, I always wanted to thank her. The action was so graceful and inclusively benign.

She was one of the few gentlewomen I have ever known, and has remained throughout my life the measure of what a human being can be.

Momma had a strange relationship with her. Most often when she passed on the road in front of the Store, she spoke to Momma in that soft yet carrying voice, "Good day, Mrs. Henderson." Momma responded with "How you, Sister Flowers?"

Mrs. Flowers didn't belong to our church, nor was she Momma's familiar. Why on earth did she insist on calling her Sister Flowers? Shame made me want to hide my face. Mrs. Flowers deserved better than to be called Sister. Then, Momma left out the verb. Why not ask, "How *are* you, *Mrs.* Flowers?" With the unbalanced passion of the young, I hated her for showing her ignorance to Mrs. Flowers. It didn't occur to me for many years that they were as alike as sisters, separated only by formal education.

Although I was upset, neither of the women was in the least shaken by what I thought an unceremonious greeting. Mrs. Flowers would continue her easy gait up the hill to her little bungalow, and Momma kept on shelling peas or doing whatever had brought her to the front porch. . . .

[Mrs. Flowers] appealed to me because she was like people I had never met personally. Like women in English novels who walked the moors (whatever they were) with their loyal dogs racing at a respectful distance. Like the women who sat in front of roaring fireplaces, drinking tea incessantly from silver trays full of scones and crumpets. Women who walked over the "heath" and read morocco-bound books and had two last names divided by a hyphen. It would be safe to say that she made me proud to be Negro, just by being herself.

She acted just as refined as whitefolks in the movies and books and she was more beautiful, for none of them could have come near that warm color without looking gray by comparison.

It was fortunate that I never saw her in the company of powhitefolks. For since they tend to think of their whiteness as an evenizer, I'm certain that I would have had to hear her spoken to commonly as Bertha, and my image of her would have been shattered like the unmendable Humpty-Dumpty.

One summer afternoon, sweet-milk fresh in my memory, she stopped at the Store to buy provisions. Another Negro woman of her health and age would have been expected to carry the paper sacks home in one hand, but Momma said, "Sister Flowers, I'll send Bailey up to your house with these things."

She smiled that slow dragging smile, "Thank you, Mrs. Henderson. I'd prefer Marguerite, though." My name was beautiful when she said it. "I've been meaning to talk to her, anyway." They gave each other age-group looks.

Momma said, "Well, that's all right then. Sister, go and change your dress. You going to Sister Flowers's."

The chifforobe was a maze. What on earth did one put on to go to Mrs. Flowers' house? I knew I shouldn't put on a Sunday dress. It might be sacrilegious. Certainly not a house dress, since I was already wearing a fresh one. I chose a school dress, naturally. It was formal without suggesting that going to Mrs. Flowers' house was equivalent to attending church.

I trusted myself back into the Store.

"Now, don't you look nice." I had chosen the right thing, for once.

"Mrs. Henderson, you make most of the children's clothes, don't you?"

"Yes, ma'am. Sure do. Store-bought clothes ain't hardly worth the thread it take to stitch them."

"I'll say you do a lovely job, though, so neat. That dress looks professional."

Momma was enjoying the seldom-received compliments. Since everyone we knew (except Mrs. Flowers, of course) could sew competently, praise was rarely handed out for the commonly practiced craft.

"I try, with the help of the Lord, Sister Flowers, to finish the inside just like I does the outside. Come here, Sister."

I had buttoned up the collar and tied the belt, apronlike, in back. Momma told me to turn around. With one hand she pulled the strings and the belt fell free at both sides of my waist. Then her large hands were at my neck, opening the button loops. I was terrified. What was happening?

"Take it off, Sister." She had her hands on the hem of the dress.

"I don't need to see the inside, Mrs. Henderson, I can tell . . ."
But the dress was over my head and my arms were stuck in the
sleeves. Momma said, "That'll do. See here, Sister Flowers, I French-
seams around the armholes." Through the cloth film, I saw the
shadow approach. "That makes it last longer. Children these days
would bust out of sheet-metal clothes. They so rough."

"That is a very good job, Mrs. Henderson. You should be proud.
You can put your dress back on, Marguerite."

"No ma'am. Pride is a sin. And 'cording to the Good Book, it
goeth before a fall."

"That's right. So the Bible says. It's a good thing to keep in mind."

I wouldn't look at either of them. Momma hadn't thought that
taking off my dress in front of Mrs. Flowers would kill me stone
dead. If I had refused, she would have thought I was trying to be
"womanish" and might have remembered St. Louis. Mrs. Flowers
had known that I would be embarrassed and that was even worse.
I picked up the groceries and went out to wait in the hot sunshine.
It would be fitting if I got a sunstroke and died before they came
outside. Just dropped dead on the slanting porch.

There was a little path beside the rocky road, and Mrs. Flowers
walked in front swinging her arms and picking her way over the
stones.

She said, without turning her head, to me, "I hear you're doing
very good school work, Marguerite, but that it's all written. The
teachers report that they have trouble getting you to talk in class."
We passed the triangular farm on our left and the path widened to
allow us to walk together. I hung back in the separate unasked and
unanswerable questions.

"Come and walk along with me, Marguerite." I couldn't have
refused even if I wanted to. She pronounced my name so nicely.
Or more correctly, she spoke each word with such clarity that I
was certain a foreigner who didn't understand English could have
understood her.

"Now no one is going to make you talk—possibly no one can.
But bear in mind, language is man's way of communicating with his

fellow man and it is language alone which separates him from the lower animals." That was a totally new idea to me, and I would need time to think about it.

"Your grandmother says you read a lot. Every chance you get. That's good, but not good enough. Words mean more than what is set down on paper. It takes the human voice to infuse them with the shades of deeper meaning."

I memorized the part about the human voice infusing words. It seemed so valid and poetic.

She said she was going to give me some books and that I not only must read them, I must read them aloud. She suggested that I try to make a sentence sound in as many different ways as possible.

"I'll accept no excuse if you return a book to me that has been badly handled." My imagination boggled at the punishment I would deserve if in fact I did abuse a book of Mrs. Flowers'. Death would be too kind and brief.

The odors in the house surprised me. Somehow I had never connected Mrs. Flowers with food or eating or any other common experience of common people. There must have been an outhouse, too, but my mind never recorded it.

The sweet scent of vanilla had met us as she opened the door.

"I made tea cookies this morning. You see, I had planned to invite you for cookies and lemonade so we could have this little chat. The lemonade is in the icebox."

It followed that Mrs. Flowers would have ice on an ordinary day, when most families in our town bought ice late on Saturdays only a few times during the summer to be used in the wooden ice-cream freezers.

She took the bags from me and disappeared through the kitchen door. I looked around the room that I had never in my wildest fantasies imagined I would see. Browned photographs leered or threatened from the wall and the white, freshly done curtains pushed against themselves and against the wind. I wanted to gobble up the room entire and take it to Bailey, who would help me analyze and enjoy it.

"Have a seat, Marguerite. Over there by the table." She carried a platter covered with a tea towel. Although she warned that she hadn't tried her hand at baking sweets for some time, I was certain that like everything else about her the cookies would be perfect.

They were flat round wafers, slightly browned on the edges and butter-yellow in the center. With the cold lemonade they were sufficient for childhood's lifelong diet. Remembering my manners, I took nice little lady-like bites off the edges. She said she had made them expressly for me and that she had a few in the kitchen that I could take home to my brother. So I jammed one whole cake in my mouth and the rough crumbs scratched the insides of my jaws, and if I hadn't had to swallow, it would have been a dream come true.

As I ate she began the first of what we later called "my lessons in living." She said that I must always be intolerant of ignorance but understanding of illiteracy. That some people, unable to go to school, were more educated and even more intelligent than college professors. She encouraged me to listen carefully to what country people called mother wit. That in those homely sayings was couched the collective wisdom of generations.

When I finished the cookies she brushed off the table and brought a thick, small book from the bookcase. I had read *A Tale of Two Cities* and found it up to my standards as a romantic novel. She opened the first page and I heard poetry for the first time in my life.

"It was the best of times and the worst of times . . ." Her voice slid in and curved down through and over the words. She was nearly singing. I wanted to look at the pages. Were they the same that I had read? Or were there notes, music, lined on the pages, as in a hymn book? Her sounds began cascading gently. I knew from listening to a thousand preachers that she was nearing the end of her reading, and I hadn't really heard, heard to understand, a single word.

"How do you like that?"

It occurred to me that she expected a response. The sweet vanilla flavor was still on my tongue and her reading was a wonder in my ears. I had to speak.

I said, "Yes, ma'am." It was the least I could do, but it was the most also.

"There's one more thing. Take this book of poems and memorize one for me. Next time you pay me a visit, I want you to recite."

I have tried often to search behind the sophistication of years for the enchantment I so easily found in those gifts. The essence escapes but its aura remains. To be allowed, no, invited, into the private lives of strangers, and to share the joys and fears, was a chance to exchange the Southern bitter wormwood for a cup of mead with Beowulf or a hot cup of tea and milk with Oliver Twist. When I said aloud, "It is a far, far better thing that I do, than I have ever done . . ." tears of love filled my eyes at my selflessness.

On that first day, I ran down the hill and into the road (few cars ever came along it) and had the good sense to stop running before I reached the Store.

I was liked, and what a difference it made. I was respected not as Mrs. Henderson's grandchild or Bailey's sister but for just being Marguerite Johnson.

Childhood's logic never asks to be proved (all conclusions are absolute). I didn't question why Mrs. Flowers had singled me out for attention, nor did it occur to me that Momma might have asked her to give me a little talking to. All I cared about was that she had made tea cookies for *me* and had read to *me* from her favorite book. It was enough to prove that she liked me.

Morehouse College

MARTIN LUTHER KING JR.

Fascinated by the idea of refusing to cooperate
with an evil system, I was so deeply moved
that I reread the work several times.

Rev. Dr. Martin Luther King Jr. (1929–1968) has been highly regarded
as the foremost leader of the American civil rights movement. At age
twenty-six, he came to prominence in 1955 with the Montgomery bus
boycott, which he led in protest of the arrest of seamstress Rosa Parks
for resisting a bus driver's order to relinquish her seat in the segregated
colored section to a White man. The 381-day protest ended with a
United States district court order that desegregated public transpor-
tation systems in Alabama, and was affirmed by the United States
Supreme Court, effectively ruling such discrimination unconstitutional
throughout the country. Imprisoned under horrific conditions in 1963,
he began writing in the margins of a newspaper "Letter from Birming-
ham Jail," which became an important part of his book *Why We Can't
Wait*. For his continuing leadership, informed by his religious beliefs
as a Baptist minister using nonviolence as a strategic tactic, King was
awarded the Nobel Peace Prize in 1964. His optimistic and inspirational
"I Have a Dream" speech, delivered at the 1963 March on Washington
he co-organized, is one of the world's most famous orations.

In this excerpt from his autobiography, King gives us insight into
his college years—that precious time between childhood and adulthood
when philosophies and beliefs become ingrained—and how the books
he read during those years influenced the great man he would become.

At the age of fifteen, I entered Morehouse College. My father and my maternal grandfather had also attended, so Morehouse has had three generations of Kings.

I shall never forget the hardships that I had upon entering college, for though I had been one of the top students in high school, I was still reading at only an eighth-grade level. I went to college from the eleventh grade. I never went to the twelfth grade, and skipped another grade earlier, so I was a pretty young fellow at Morehouse.

My days in college were very exciting ones. There was a free atmosphere at Morehouse, and it was there I had my first frank discussion on race. The professors were not caught up in the clutches of state funds and could teach what they wanted with academic freedom. They encouraged us in a positive quest for a solution to racial ills. I realized that nobody there was afraid. Important people came in to discuss the race problem rationally with us.

When I went to Morehouse as a freshman in 1944, my concern for racial and economic justice was already substantial. During my student days I read Henry David Thoreau's essay "On Civil Disobedience" for the first time. Here, in this courageous New Englander's refusal to pay his taxes and his choice of jail rather than support a war that would spread slavery's territory into Mexico, I made my first contact with the theory of nonviolent resistance. Fascinated by the idea of refusing to cooperate with an evil system, I was so deeply moved that I reread the work several times.

I became convinced that noncooperation with evil is as much a moral obligation as is cooperation with good. No other person has been more eloquent and passionate in getting this idea across than Henry David Thoreau. As a result of his writings and personal witness, we are the heirs of a legacy of creative protest. The teachings of Thoreau came alive in our civil rights movement; indeed, they are more alive than ever before. Whether expressed in a sit-in at lunch counters, a freedom ride into Mississippi, a peaceful protest in Albany, Georgia, a bus boycott in Montgomery, Alabama, these are outgrowths of Thoreau's insistence that evil must be resisted and that no moral man can patiently adjust to injustice.

As soon as I entered college, I started working with the organizations that were trying to make racial justice a reality. The wholesome relations we had in the Intercollegiate Council convinced me that we had many white persons as allies, particularly among the younger generation. I had been ready to resent the whole white race, but as I got to see more of white people, my resentment was softened, and a spirit of cooperation took its place. I was at the point where I was deeply interested in political matters and social ills. I could envision myself playing a part in breaking down the legal barriers to Negro rights.

"An inner urge calling me to serve society"

Because of the influence of my mother and father, I guess I always had a deep urge to serve humanity, but I didn't start out with an interest to enter the ministry. I thought I could probably do it better as a lawyer or doctor. One of my closest friends at Morehouse, Walter McCall, was clear about his intention of going into the ministry, but I was slow to make up my mind. I did serve as assistant to my father for six months. . . .

Two men—Dr. [Benjamin] Mays, president of Morehouse college and one of the great influences in my life, and Dr. George Kelsey, a professor of philosophy and religion—made me stop and think. Both were ministers, both deeply religious, and yet both were learned men, aware of all the trends of modern thinking. I could see in their lives the ideal of what I wanted a minister to be.

It was in my senior year of college that I entered the ministry. I had felt the urge to enter the ministry from my high school days, but accumulated doubts had somewhat blocked the urge. Now it appeared again with an inescapable drive. I felt a sense of responsibility which I could not escape.

I guess the influence of my father had a great deal to do with my going into the ministry. This is not to say that he ever spoke to me in terms of being a minister but that my admiration for him was the great moving factor. He set forth a noble example that I didn't mind following. I still feel the effects of the noble moral and ethical ideals that I grew up under. They have been real and precious to me, and even in moments of theological doubt I could never turn away from them.

At the age of nineteen I finished college and was ready to enter seminary.

Crozer Seminary

Not until 1948, when I entered Crozer Theological Seminary in Chester, Pennsylvania, did I begin a serious intellectual quest for a method to eliminate social evil. I turned to a serious study of the social and ethical theories of the great philosophers, from Plato and Aristotle down to Rousseau, Hobbes, Bentham, Mill, and Locke. All of these masters stimulated my thinking—such as it was—and, while finding things to question in each of them, I nevertheless learned a great deal from their study.

I spent a great deal of time reading the work of the great social philosophers. I came early to Walter Rauschenbusch's *Christianity and the Social Crisis*, which left an indelible imprint on my thinking by giving me a theological basis for the social concern which had already grown up in me as a result of my early experiences. Of course there were points at which I differed with Rauschenbusch. I felt that he had fallen victim to the nineteenth-century "cult of inevitable progress" which led him to a superficial optimism concerning man's nature. Moreover, he came perilously close to identifying the Kingdom of God with a particular social and economic system—a tendency which should never befall the Church. But in spite of these shortcomings Rauschenbusch had done a great service for the Christian Church by insisting that the gospel deals with the whole man—not only his soul but his body; not only his spiritual well-being but his material well-being.

. . . One Sunday afternoon I traveled to Philadelphia to hear a sermon by Dr. Mordecai Johnson, president of Howard University. He was there to preach for the Fellowship House of Philadelphia. Dr. Johnson had just returned from a trip to India, and, to my great interest, he spoke of the life and teachings of Mahatma Gandhi. His message was so profound and electrifying that I left the meeting and bought a half-dozen books on Gandhi's life and works.

Like most people, I had heard of Gandhi, but I had never studied him seriously. As I read I became deeply fascinated by his campaigns of nonviolent resistance. I was particularly moved by his Salt March to the Sea and his numerous fasts. The whole concept of *Satyagraha* (*Satya* is truth which equals love, and *agraha* is force; *Satyagraha*, therefore, means truth force or love force) was profoundly significant to me. As I delved deeper into the philosophy of Gandhi, my skepticism concerning the power of love gradually diminished, and I came to see for the first time its potency in the area of social reform. Prior to reading Gandhi, I had about concluded that the ethics of Jesus were only effective in individual relationships. The "turn the other cheek" philosophy and the "love your enemies" philosophy were only valid, I felt, when individuals were in conflict with other individuals; when racial groups and nations were in conflict a more realistic approach seemed necessary. But after reading Gandhi, I saw how utterly mistaken I was.

Gandhi was probably the first person in history to lift the love ethic of Jesus above mere interaction between individuals to a powerful and effective social force on a large scale. Love for Gandhi was a potent instrument for social and collective transformation. It was in this Gandhian emphasis on love and nonviolence that I discovered the method for social reform that I had been seeking. The intellectual and moral satisfaction that I failed to gain from the utilitarianism of Bentham and Mill, the revolutionary methods of Marx and Lenin, the social contracts theory of Hobbes, the "back to nature" optimism of Rousseau, the superman philosophy of Nietzsche, I found in the nonviolent resistance philosophy of Gandhi.

The Site of Memory

TONI MORRISON

Literacy was power, a way of assuming and proving
the "humanity" that the Constitution denied them.

Chloe Anthony "Toni" Wofford Morrison was born in Lorain, Ohio, in
1931. The author of eleven novels, from *The Bluest Eye* (1970) to *God
Help the Child* (2015), and several books for children, she is the recipient of the National Book Critics Circle Award for *Song of Solomon* and
the Pulitzer Prize for Fiction for *Beloved*. In 1993, she became the first
African American woman to be awarded the Nobel Prize in Literature,
and, in 2012, President Barack Obama presented her with the Presidential Medal of Freedom. She serves as professor emeritus at Princeton
University, where she taught for seventeen years after working as a book
editor at Random House.

Still providing inspiration for writers, Morrison wrote in a 2013 Twit-
ter post that has been widely quoted: "If there's a book that you want to
read, but it hasn't been written yet, then you must write it."

Here, in an essay adapted from an interview published in *What Moves
at the Margin: Selected Nonfiction by Toni Morrison*, originally appearing
in *Inventing the Truth: The Art and Craft of Memoir*, Morrison discusses
the origins of Black literature, the critical job of the Black writer now,
and the devastating personal loss that led to the characterizations in
Song of Solomon.

n this country the print origins of black literature (as distinguished from the oral origins) were slave narratives. These book-length narratives (autobiographies, recollections, memoirs), of which well over a hundred were published, are familiar texts to historians and students of black history. They range from the adventure-packed life of Olaudah Equiano's *The Interesting Narrative of the Life of Olaudah Equiano, or Gustavus Vassa, the African, Written by Himself* (1769) to the quiet desperation of *Incidents in the Life of a Slave Girl: Written by Herself* (1861), in which Harriet Jacobs ("Linda Brent") records hiding for seven years in a room too small to stand up in; from the political savvy of Frederick Douglass's *Narrative of the Life of Frederick Douglass, an American Slave, Written by Himself* (1845) to the subtlety and modesty of Henry Bibb, whose voice, in *Life and Adventures of Henry Bibb, an American Slave, Written by Himself* (1849), is surrounded by ("loaded with" is a better phrase) documents attesting to its authenticity. Bibb is careful to note that his formal schooling (three weeks) was short, but that he was "educated in the school of adversity, whips, and chains." Born in Kentucky, he put aside his plans to escape in order to marry. But when he learned that he was the father of a slave and watched the degradation of his wife and child, he reactivated those plans.

Whatever the style and circumstances of these narratives, they were written to say principally two things. One: "This is my historical life—my singular, special example that is personal, but that also represents the race." Two: "I write this text to persuade other people—you, the reader, who is probably not black—that we are human beings worthy of God's grace and the immediate abandonment of slavery." With these two missions in mind, the narratives were clearly pointed.

In Equiano's account, the purpose is quite up-front. Born in 1745 near the Niger River and captured at the age of ten, he survived the Middle Passage, American plantation slavery, wars in Canada and the Mediterranean; learned navigation and clerking from a Quaker named Robert King, and bought his freedom at twenty-one. He lived as a free servant, traveling widely and living most of his latter life in England. Here he is speaking to the British without equivocation: "I hope to have the satisfaction of seeing the renovation of liberty and justice resting on the British government. . . . I hope and expect the attention of gentlemen of power. . . . May the time come—at least the speculation is to me pleasing—when the sable people shall gratefully commemorate the auspicious era of extensive freedom." With typically eighteenth-century reticence he records his singular and representative life for one purpose: to change things. In fact, he and his co-authors *did* change things. Their works gave fuel to the fires that abolitionists were setting everywhere.

More difficult was getting the fair appraisal of literary critics. The writings of church martyrs and confessors are and were read for the eloquence of their message as well as their experience of redemption, but the American slaves' autobiographical narratives were frequently scorned as "biased," "inflammatory" and "improbable." These attacks are particularly difficult to understand in view of the fact that it was extremely important, as you can imagine, for the writers of these narratives to appear as objective as possible—not to offend the reader by being too angry, or by showing too much outrage, or by calling the reader names. As recently as 1966, Paul Edward, who edited and abridged Equiano's story, praises the narrative for its refusal to be "inflammatory."

"As a rule," Edwards writes, "he [Equiano] puts no emotional pressure on the reader other than that which the situation itself contains—his language does not strain after our sympathy, but expects it to be given naturally and at the proper time. This quiet avoidance of emotional display produces many of the best passages in the book." Similarly, an 1836 review of Charles Bell's *Life and Adventures of a Fugitive Slave*, which appeared in the *Quarterly Anti-Slavery Magazine*, praised Bell's account for its objectivity. "We rejoice in the book the more, because it is not a partisan work. . . . It broaches no theory in regard to [slavery], nor proposes any mode or time of emancipation."

As determined as the black writers were to persuade the reader of the evil of slavery, they also complimented him by assuming his nobility of heart and his high-mindedness. They tried to summon up his finer nature in order to encourage him to employ it. They knew that their readers were the people who could make a difference in terminating slavery. Their stories—of brutality, adversity and deliverance—had great popularity in spite of critical hostility in many quarters and patronizing sympathy in others. There was a time when the hunger for "slave stories" was difficult to quiet, as sales figures show. Douglass's *Narrative* sold five thousand copies in four months; by 1847 it had sold eleven thousand copies. Equiano's book had thirty-six editions between 1789 and 1850. Moses Roper's book had ten editions from 1837 to 1856; William Wells Brown's was reprinted four times in its first year. Solomon Northrop's [*sic*] book sold twenty-seven thousand copies before two years had passed. A book by Josiah Henson (argued by some to be the model for the "Tom" of Harriet Beecher Stowe's *Uncle Tom's Cabin*) had a pre-publication sale of five thousand.

In addition to using their own lives to expose the horrors of slavery, they had a companion motive for their efforts. The prohibition against teaching a slave to read and write (which in many Southern states carried severe punishment) and against a slave's learning to read and write had to be scuttled at all costs. These writers knew that literacy was power. Voting, after all, was inextricably connected to the ability to read; literacy was a way of assuming and proving the "humanity" that the Constitution denied them. That is why the narratives carry the subtitle "written by himself," or "herself," and include introductions and prefaces by white sympathizers to authenticate them. Other narratives, "edited by" such well-known anti-slavery figures as Lydia Maria Child and John Greenleaf Whittier contain prefaces to assure the reader how little editing was needed. A literate slave was supposed to be a contradiction in terms.

One has to remember that the climate in which they write reflected not only the Age of Enlightenment but its twin, born at the same time, the Age of Scientific Racism. David Hume, Immanuel

Kant and Thomas Jefferson, to mention only a few, had documented their conclusions that blacks were incapable of intelligence. Frederick Douglass knew otherwise, and he wrote refutations of what Jefferson said in "Notes on the State of Virginia": "Never yet could I find that a black had uttered a thought above the level of plain narration, never see even an elementary trait of painting or sculpture." A sentence that I have always thought ought to be engraved at the door to the Rockefeller Collection of African Art. Hegel, in 1813, had said that Africans had no "history" and couldn't write in modern languages. Kant disregarded a perceptive observation by a black man by saying, "This fellow was quite black from head to foot, a clear proof that what he said was stupid."

Yet no slave society in the history of the world wrote more— or more thoughtfully—about its own enslavement. The milieu, however, dictated the purpose and the style. The narratives are instructive, moral and obviously representative. Some of them are patterned after the sentimental novel that was in vogue at the time. But whatever the level of eloquence or the form, popular taste discouraged the writers from dwelling too long or too carefully on the more sordid details of their experience. Whenever there was an unusually violent incident, or a scatological one, or something "excessive," one finds the writer taking refuge in the literary conventions of the day. "I was left in a state of distraction not to be described" (Equiano). "But let us now leave the rough usage of the field . . . and turn our attention to the less repulsive slave life as it existed in the house of my childhood" (Douglass). "I am not about to harrow the feelings of my readers by a terrific representation of the untold horrors of that fearful system of oppression. . . . It is not my purpose to descend deeply into the dark and noisome caverns of the hell of slavery" (Henry Box Brown).

Over and over, the writers pull the narrative up short with a phrase such as, "But let us drop a veil over these proceedings too terrible to relate." In shaping the experience to make it palatable to those who were in a position to alleviate it, they were silent about many things, and they "forgot" many other things. There was a care-

ful selection of the instances that they would record and a careful
rendering of those that they chose to describe. Lydia Maria Child
identified the problem in her introduction to "Linda Brent's" tale of
sexual abuse: "I am well aware that many will accuse me of indeco-
rum for presenting these pages to the public; for the experiences of
this intelligent and much-injured woman belong to a class which
some call delicate subjects, and others indelicate. This peculiar phase
of Slavery has generally been kept veiled; but the public ought to be
made acquainted with its monstrous features, and I'm willing to take
the responsibility of presenting them with the veil drawn [aside]."

But most importantly—at least for me—there was no mention
of their interior life.

For me—a writer in the last quarter of the twentieth century, not
much more than a hundred years after Emancipation, a writer who is
black and a woman—the exercise is very different. My job becomes
how to rip that veil drawn over "proceedings too terrible to relate."
The exercise is also critical for any person who is black, or who belongs to any marginalized category, for historically, we were seldom
invited to participate in the discourse even when we were its topic.

Moving that veil aside requires, therefore, certain things. First
of all, I must trust my own recollections. I must also depend on
the recollections of others. Thus, memory weighs heavily in what I
write, in how I begin and in what I find to be significant. Zora Neale
Hurston said, "Like the dead-seeming cold rocks, I have memories
within that came out of the material that went to make me." These
"memories within" are the subsoil of my work. But memories and
recollections won't give me total access to the unwritten interior life
of these people. Only the act of the imagination can help me.

If writing is thinking and discovery and selection and order and
meaning, it is also awe and reverence and mystery and magic. I
suppose I could dispense with the last four if I were not so deadly
serious about fidelity to the milieu out of which I write and in which
my ancestors actually lived. Infidelity to that milieu—the absence
of the interior life, the deliberate excising of it from the records that

the slaves themselves told—is precisely the problem in the discourse that proceeded without us. How I gain access to that interior life is what drives me and is the part of this talk which both distinguishes my fiction from autobiographical strategies and which also embraces certain autobiographical strategies. It's a kind of literary archeology: on the basis of some information and a little bit of guesswork you journey to a site to see what remains were left behind and to reconstruct the world that these remains imply. What makes it fiction is the nature of the imaginative act; my reliance on the image—on the remains—in addition to recollection, to yield up a kind of a truth. By "image," of course, I don't mean "symbol"; I simply mean "picture" and the feelings that accompany the picture.

Fiction, by definition, is distinct from fact. Presumably it's the product of imagination—invention—and it claims the freedom to dispense with "what really happened," or where it really happened, or when it really happened, and nothing in it needs to be publicly verifiable, although much in it can be verified. By contrast, the scholarship of the biographer and the literary critic seems to us only trustworthy when the events of fiction can be traced to some publicly verifiable fact. It's the research of the "Oh, yes, this is where he or she got it from" school, which gets its own credibility from excavating the credibility of the sources of the imagination, not the nature of the imagination.

The work that I do frequently falls, in the minds of most people, into that realm of fiction called fantastic, or mythic, or magical, or unbelievable. I'm not comfortable with these labels. I consider that my single gravest responsibility (in spite of that magic) is not to lie. When I hear someone say, "Truth is stranger than fiction," I think that old chestnut is truer than we know, because it doesn't say that truth is truer than fiction; just that it's stranger, meaning that it's odd. It may be excessive, it may be more interesting, but the important thing is that it's random—and fiction is not random.

Therefore the crucial distinction for me is not the difference between fact and fiction, but the distinction between fact and truth. Because facts can exist without human intelligence, but truth cannot. So I'm looking to find and expose a truth about the interior life of people who didn't write it (which doesn't mean that they didn't have it); if I'm trying to fill in the blanks that the slave narratives left—to part the veil that was so frequently drawn, to implement the stories that I heard—then the approach that's most productive and most trustworthy for me is the recollection that moves from the image to the text. Not from the text to the image.

Simone de Beauvoir, in *A Very Easy Death*, says, "I don't know why I was so shocked by my mother's death." When she heard her mother's name being called at the funeral by the priest, she says, "Emotion seized me by the throat . . . 'Françoise de Beauvoir': the words brought her to life; they summed up her history, from birth to marriage to widowhood to the grave. Françoise de Beauvoir—that retiring woman, so rarely named, became an *important* person." The book becomes an exploration both into her own grief and into the images in which the grief lay buried.

Unlike Mme. de Beauvoir, Frederick Douglass asks the reader's patience for spending about half a page on the death of his grandmother—easily the most profound loss he had suffered—and he apologizes by saying, in effect, "It really was very important to me. I hope you aren't bored by my indulgence." He makes no attempt to explore that death: its images or its meaning. His narrative is as close to factual as he can make it, which leaves no room for subjective speculation. James Baldwin, on the other hand, in *Notes of a Native Son*, says, in recording his father's life and his own relationship to his father, "All of my father's Biblical texts and songs, which I had decided were meaningless, were ranged before me at his death like empty bottles, waiting to hold the meaning which life would give them for me." And then his text fills those bottles. Like Simone de Beauvoir, he moves from the event to the image that it left. My route is the reverse: the image comes first and tells me what the "memory" is about.

I can't tell you how I felt when my father died. But I was able to write *Song of Solomon* and imagine, not him, and not his specific interior life, but the world that he inhabited and the private or interior life of the people in it. And I can't tell you how I felt reading to my grandmother while she was turning over and over in her bed (because she was dying, and she was not comfortable), but I could try to reconstruct the world that she lived in. And I have suspected, more often than not, that I *know* more than she did, that I *know* more than my grandfather and my great-grandmother did, but I also know that I'm no wiser than they were. And whenever I have tried earnestly to diminish their vision and prove to myself that I know more, and when I have tried to speculate on their interior life and match it up with my own, I have been overwhelmed every time by the richness of theirs compared to my own. Like Frederick Douglass talking about his grandmother, and James Baldwin talking about his father, and Simone de Beauvoir talking about her mother, these people are my access to me; they are my entrance into my own interior life. Which is why the images that float around them—the remains, so to speak, at the archeological site—surface first, and they surface so vividly and so compellingly that I acknowledge them as my route to a reconstruction of a world, to an exploration of an interior life that was not written and to the revelation of a kind of truth.

So the nature of my research begins with something as ineffable and as flexible as a dimly recalled figure, the corner of a room, a voice. I began to write my second book, which was called *Sula*, because of my preoccupation with a picture of a woman and the way in which I heard her name pronounced. Her name was Hannah, and I think she was a friend of my mother's. I don't remember seeing her very much, but what I do remember is the color around her—a kind of violet, a suffusion of something violet—and her eyes, which appeared to be half closed. But what I remember most is how the women said her name: how they said "Hannah Peace" and smiled to themselves, and there was some secret about her that they knew, which they didn't talk about, at least not in my hearing, but it seemed *loaded* in the way in which they said her name. And I suspected that she was a little bit of an outlaw but that they approved in some way.

And then, thinking about their relationship to her and the way in which they talked about her, the way in which they articulated her name, made me think about friendship between women. What is it that they forgive each other for? And what it is that is unforgiveable in the world of women. I don't want to know any more about Miss Hannah Peace, and I'm not going to ask my mother who she really was and what did she do and what were you laughing about and why were you smiling? Because my experience when I do this with my mother is so crushing: she will give you *the* most pedestrian information you ever heard, and I would like to keep all of my remains and my images intact in their mystery when I begin. Later I will get to the facts. That way I can explore two worlds—the actual and the possible.

What I want to do is to track an image from picture to meaning to text—a journey which appears in the novel that I'm writing now, which is called *Beloved*.

I'm trying to write a particular kind of scene, and I see corn on the cob. To "see" corn on the cob doesn't mean that it suddenly hovers; it only means that it keeps coming back. And in trying to figure out "What is all this corn doing?" I discover what it *is* doing.

I see the house where I grew up in Lorain, Ohio. My parents had a garden some distance away from our house, and they didn't welcome me and my sister there, when we were young, because we were not able to distinguish between the things that they wanted to grow and the things that they didn't, so we were not able to hoe, or weed, until much later.

I see them walking, together, away from me. I'm looking at their backs and what they're carrying in their arms: their tools, and maybe a peck basket. Sometimes when they walk away from me they hold hands, and they go to this other place in the garden. They have to cross some railroad tracks to get there.

I am also aware that my mother and father sleep at odd hours because my father works many jobs and works at night. And these naps are times of pleasure for me and my sister because nobody's giving us chores, or telling us what to do, or nagging us in any way. In addition to which, there is some feeling of pleasure in them that I'm only vaguely aware of. They're very rested when they take these naps.

And later on in the summer we have an opportunity to eat corn, which is the one plant that I can distinguish from the others, and which is the harvest that I like the best; the others are the food that no child likes—the collards, the okra, the strong, violent vegetables that I would give a great deal for now. But I do like the corn because it's sweet, and because we all sit down to eat it, and it's finger food, and it's hot, and it's even good cold, and there are neighbors in, and there are uncles in, and it's easy, and it's nice.

The picture of the corn and the nimbus of emotion surrounding it became a powerful one in the manuscript I'm now completing.

Authors arrive at text and subtext in thousands of ways, learning each time they begin anew how to recognize a valuable idea and how to render the texture that accompanies, reveals or displays it to its best advantage. The process by which this is accomplished is endlessly fascinating to me. I have always thought that as an editor for twenty years I understood writers better than their most careful critics, because in examining the manuscript in each of its subsequent stages I knew the author's process, how his or her mind worked, what was effortless, what took time, where the "solution" to a problem came from. The end result—the book—was all that the critic had to go on.

Still, for me, that was the least important aspect of the work. Because, no matter how "fictional" the account of these writers, or how much it was a product of invention, the act of imagination is bound up with memory. You know, they straightened out the Mississippi River in places, to make room for houses and livable acreage. Occasionally the river floods these places. "Floods" is the word they use, but in fact it is not flooding; it is remembering. Remembering where it used to be. All water has a perfect memory and is forever trying to get back to where it was. Writers are like that: remembering where we were, what valley we ran through, what the banks were like, the light that was there and the route back to our original place. It is emotional memory—what the nerves and the skin remember as well as how it appeared. And a rush of imagination is our "flooding."

Along with personal recollection, the matrix of the work I do is
the wish to extend, fill in and complement slave autobiographical
narratives. But only the matrix. What comes of all that is dictated by
other concerns, not least among them the novel's own integrity. Still,
like water, I remember where I was before I was "straightened out."

Where Are the People of Color in Children's Books?

WALTER DEAN MYERS

I realized exactly what I wanted to do when I wrote
about poor inner-city children—to make them human
in the eyes of readers and, especially, in their own
eyes, to make them feel as if they are part of America's
dream, and that they are wanted in this country.

Walter Dean Myers (1937–2014) wrote more than 110 books for children and young adults. In 1969, he won the Council on Interracial Books for Children contest, which resulted in the publication of his first book, *Where Does the Day Go?* He went on to win more awards than any author for young adults, including the Margaret A. Edwards Award for lifetime achievement, the Coretta Scott King Award five times, and two Newbery Honors. His book *Monster* was the first winner of the Michael L. Printz Award, a National Book Award Finalist, and a *New York Times* bestseller. In 2012, he was appointed as the National Ambassador for Young People's Literature, a post appointed by the Library of Congress to raise national awareness of the importance of lifelong literacy and education, in which he traveled around the United States promoting the slogan "Reading Is Not Optional."

In this essay, his last published work, which appeared in the *New York Times* just three months before his passing, he shares how books helped him discover who he was as a Black teenager in a White-dominated world, and why we still need diverse children's books.

Reading came early to me, but I didn't think of the words as anything special. I don't think my stepmom thought of what she was doing as more than spending time with me in our small Harlem apartment. From my comfortable perch on her lap I watched as she moved her finger slowly across the page. She probably read at about the third grade level, but that was good enough for the True Romance magazines she read. I didn't understand what the stories were about, what "bosom" meant or how someone's heart could be "broken." To me it was just the comfort of leaning against Mama and imagining the characters and what they were doing.

Later, when my sisters brought home comic books, I got Mama to read them to me, too. The magazines and comics pushed me along the road of the imaginative process. When I got my first books—"The Little Engine That Could," "Bible Stories for Every Day," and "Goldilocks and the Three Bears"—I used them on the same journeys. In the landscape of my mind I labored as hard as I could to get up the hill. I stood on the plain next to David as he fought Goliath, and tasted the porridge with Goldilocks.

As a teenager I romped the forests with Robin Hood, and trembled to the sound of gunfire with Henry in "The Red Badge of Courage." Later, when Mama's problems began to overwhelm her, I wrestled with the demons of dealing with one's mother with Stephen Dedalus in "A Portrait of the Artist as a Young Man." But by then I was beginning the quest for my own identity. To an extent I found who I was in the books I read. I was a person who felt the drama of great pain and greater joys, whose emotions could soar within the five-act structure of a Shakespearean play, or find quiet comfort in the poems of Gabriela Mistral. Every book was a landscape upon which I was free to wander.

In the dark times, when my uncle was murdered, when my family became dysfunctional with alcohol and grief, or when I realized that our economics would not allow me to go to college, I began to despair. I read voraciously, spending days in Central Park reading when I should have been going to school.

But there was something missing. I needed more than the characters in the Bible to identify with, or even the characters in Arthur Miller's plays or my beloved Balzac. As I discovered who I was, a black teenager in a white-dominated world, I saw that these characters, these lives, were not mine. I didn't want to become the "black" representative, or some shining example of diversity. What I wanted, needed really, was to become an integral and valued part of the mosaic that I saw around me.

Books did not become my enemies. They were more like friends with whom I no longer felt comfortable. I stopped reading. I stopped going to school. On my 17th birthday, I joined the Army. In retrospect I see that I had lost the potential person I would become—an odd idea that I could not have articulated at the time, but that seems so clear today.

My post-Army days became dreadful, a drunken stumble through life, with me holding on just enough to survive. Fueled by the shortest and most meaningful conversation I had ever had in a school hallway, with the one English teacher in my high school, Stuyvesant, who knew I was going to drop out, I began to write short columns for a local tabloid, and racy stories for men's magazines. Seeing my name in print helped. A little.

Then I read a story by James Baldwin: "Sonny's Blues." I didn't love the story, but I was lifted by it, for it took place in Harlem, and it was a story concerned with black people like those I knew. By humanizing the people who were like me, Baldwin's story also humanized me. The story gave me a permission that I didn't know I needed, the permission to write about my own landscape, my own map.

During my only meeting with Baldwin, at City College, I blurted out to him what his story had done for me. "I know exactly what you mean," he said. "I had to leave Harlem and the United States to search for who I was. Isn't that a shame?"

When I left Baldwin that day I felt elated that I had met a writer

I had so admired, and that we had had a shared experience. But later I realized how much more meaningful it would have been to have known Baldwin's story at 15, or at 14. Perhaps even younger, before I had started my subconscious quest for identity.

Today I am a writer, but I also see myself as something of a landscape artist. I paint pictures of scenes for inner-city youth that are familiar, and I people the scenes with brothers and aunts and friends they all have met. Thousands of young people have come to me saying that they love my books for some reason or the other, but I strongly suspect that what they have found in my pages is the same thing I found in "Sonny's Blues." They have been struck by the recognition of themselves in the story, a validation of their existence as human beings, an acknowledgment of their value by someone who understands who they are. It is the shock of recognition at its highest level.

I've reached an age at which I find myself not only examining and weighing my life's work, but thinking about how I will pass the baton so that those things I find important will continue. In 1969, when I first entered the world of writing children's literature, the field was nearly empty. Children of color were not represented, nor were children from the lower economic classes. Today, when about 40 percent of public school students nationwide are black and Latino, the disparity of representation is even more egregious. In the middle of the night I ask myself if anyone really cares.

When I was doing research for my book "Monster," I approached a white lawyer doing pro bono work in the courts defending poor clients. I said that it must be difficult to get witnesses to court to testify on behalf of an inner-city client, and he replied that getting witnesses was not as difficult as it sometimes appeared on television. "The trouble," he said, "is to humanize my clients in the eyes of a jury. To make them think of this defendant as a human being and not just one of 'them.' "

I realized that this was exactly what I wanted to do when I wrote about poor inner-city children—to make them human in the eyes of readers and, especially, in their own eyes. I need to make them feel as if they are part of America's dream, that all the rhetoric is meant for them, and that they are wanted in this country.

Years ago, I worked in the personnel office for a transformer firm. We needed to hire a chemist, and two candidates stood out, in my mind, for the position. One was a young white man with a degree from St. John's University and the other an equally qualified black man from Grambling College (now Grambling State University) in Louisiana. I proposed to the department head that we send them both to the lab and let the chief chemist make the final decision. He looked at me as if I had said something so remarkable that he was having a hard time understanding me. "You're kidding me," he said. "That black guy's no chemist."

I pointed out the degrees on the résumé that suggested otherwise, and the tension between us soared. When I confronted my superior and demanded to know what about the candidate from Grambling made him not a chemist, he grumbled something under his breath, and reluctantly sent both candidates for an interview with the chief chemist.

Simple racism, I thought. On reflection, though, I understood that I was wrong. It was racism, but not simple racism. My white co-worker had simply never encountered a black chemist before. Or a black engineer. Or a black doctor. I realized that we hired people not so much on their résumés, but rather on our preconceived notions of what the successful candidate should be like. And where was my boss going to get the notion that a chemist should be black?

Books transmit values. They explore our common humanity. What is the message when some children are not represented in those books? Where are the future white personnel managers going to get their ideas of people of color? Where are the future white loan officers and future white politicians going to get their knowledge of people of color? Where are black children going to get a sense of who they are and what they can be?

And what are the books that are being published about blacks? Joe Morton, the actor who starred in "The Brother From Another Planet," has said that all but a few motion pictures being made about blacks are about blacks as victims. In them, we are always struggling to overcome either slavery or racism. Book publishing is little better. Black history is usually depicted as folklore about slavery, and then a fast-forward to the civil rights movement. Then I'm told that black children, and boys in particular, don't read. Small wonder.

There is work to be done.

Reading for Revolution

STOKELY CARMICHAEL [KWAME TURE]

I spent hours in the library enduring the taunts of the neighbor kids about being "a bookworm." With Olympian impartiality, I read everything and anything.

"Ready for Revolution" is how Stokely Carmichael habitually answered his telephone. Born in Trinidad in 1941, Carmichael grew up in New York City, where he attended the elite Bronx High School of Science. Graduating from Howard University (where one of his young professors was Toni Morrison), he rose to prominence as a leader of the Student Nonviolent Coordinating Committee (SNCC), as an activist in the civil rights movement, and an advocate for global Pan-Africanism. In 1969, he moved to Guinea in West Africa with his wife, singer Miriam Makeba, where he served as an aide to Guinea's president Ahmed Sékou Touré, and became a student of exiled Ghanaian president Kwame Nkrumah. In honor of his mentors, he took the name Kwame Ture. He died in Guinea in 1998.

In this passage from his autobiography, *Ready for Revolution: The Life and Struggles of Stokely Carmichael [Kwame Ture]*, we learn about the parents who nurtured his quest for knowledge and the voracious reading habits that set him off on an educational path that in 1967 led him to infuse into the diasporic consciousness the inspiring philosophy and bold rallying cry of "Black Power."

One] **thing that** distanced me somewhat from much of the petty outlawry of the neighborhood guys was that I loved to read and my parents encouraged this. These were two extremely intelligent and resourceful people, but without much formal education. They were literate enough, but hardly literary. So while they were convinced of the crucial importance of reading and encouraged me in it, they could not offer much guidance about *what* to read. My mother would buy all kinds of books that seemed to her "educational." She certainly bought a lot of encyclopedias, seduced no doubt by the salesmen's line about "giving your children every educational advantage." I also spent hours in the library enduring the taunts of the neighbor kids about being "a bookworm." With Olympian impartiality, I read everything and anything.

In addition, there was the threat of punishment. My mom was the first line, the cutting edge of family discipline—my father being held in reserve for really serious offenses—and she was particularly vigilant and strict with me, the son. But as long as I stayed at or near the top of my class, she would cut me some slack. So I contrived to stay there and pretty much did. Whatever I knew would please Mother, that I tried my best to do. Anything I knew would displease her, that I'd try to avoid. For this, she has earned my undying gratitude because, without her firm restraining presence, undoubtedly I'd have ended up in jail like so many of my neighborhood buddies. Thank you, May Charles, thank you, thank you. (In Africa, when you mean to thank someone seriously, you have to do it thrice.) . . .

Bronx Science: Young Manhood

In any culture, the growth during the period from adolescence to young adulthood is of major formative importance. As American culture is organized, this growth period corresponds almost exactly to the four years of high school, which are crucial in determining not only the adult personality but one's future.

That would certainly be my experience at the Bronx High School of Science, where in the fall of '56 I was an entering freshman. At Science, I would face a number of interesting challenges—intellectual, social, cultural, political—all of which would play a significant role in my development.

Within our family, the news of my selection to Science had been greeted with quiet satisfaction, entirely as if it were no less than had been expected of me. My parents knew that Science was an "elite" school, carefully selecting and preparing the city's brightest students for college. This fit neatly with a plan being developed by my father, who in his heart had never really left his beloved Trinidad.

My father's dream was entirely consistent with his values: a family plan for both parents, me, and whichever of my four sisters wanted to sign up. The son would study medicine while the daughters would become nurses. While we children were completing our medical education, my parents would return to Trinidad, where my father would begin construction of the Carmichael family medical clinic, which he would personally design and build in preparation for the children's return to serve the community.

I guess for my father this would represent something of a triumphant homecoming: the family united and bringing back useful and necessary skills to his beloved community. Something of real and lasting value to justify his hard work in what was to him a long, cold exile. So, from that perspective, my admission to the elite Science school was right on time, clearly the first step. The extent to which we children had enthusiastically endorsed the plan can be seen in that, today, two of my sisters, Nagib and Judy, are nurses.

Bronx Science was an education in more ways than the school might have intended. I had known that the students were drawn from all five boroughs of polyglot New York and were said to be "very, very smart." So I expected high intelligence and academic rigor. But I hadn't expected—actually I hadn't given it much thought—the range of classes and cultures I found in the students there, once I got to know them.

Some were very affluent, the children of wealthy Park Avenue professionals and corporate executives. But the majority were just middle-class kids of college-educated parents, WASP, Jewish, Irish, Italian, and a few Africans born in America. Of some two thousand students at Science, about fifty or sixty were Africans from America. Some students were working class, or like me, first-generation immigrants from Asia, Africa, the Caribbean, or Latin America. That first day, the only kid I knew in the freshman class was Lefty Faronti, who was working-class Italian from my Bronx neighborhood.

———

The first challenge was academic. The one thing we all had in common was the knowledge that we were all supposed to be very smart. Naturally, I was eager to see how I would match up against New York's smartest. From the first day I could see that I was not the only freshman nervously sizing up the competition, eager for a chance to show off his smarts. And in truth, competition would be the rule at Science. It didn't take me long to understand that these whites were not necessarily any smarter than me, but that they simply—many of them—had intellectual backgrounds that I lacked.

On the first day, in one of the first classes, the first question we were asked was about our summer reading. How many books and which authors? Boy, was I glad, because I'd read a lot of books. My hand just shot up. Luckily for me, the teacher went in alphabetical order, because I was in for a shock.

I read a lot, voraciously but not at all selectively. My parents had not finished high school or studied in this country, but they knew I should read and insisted on it. But they didn't know *what* I should read. As I've said, my mom brought home tons of books, any books she concluded were "good," i.e., "educational." I read everything and anything, from *Reader's Digest* to the Hardy Boys and Horatio Alger–type uplifting books.

But these kids in the class had (or claimed to have) read authors about whom I'd never heard—Jack London, Ernest Hemingway,

William Faulkner, John Steinbeck, and even names that didn't sound American. Later I would discover that they were in fact Russian and French. For instance, if memory serves, a boy sitting immediately behind me claimed to be reading *Capital* by Karl Marx. Long before they got to me, my hand was down for I was scribbling furiously, writing down all these unknown writers whom I would read as quickly as possible, for I resolved I had to know whatever my classmates knew. I ended up with quite a reading list that first day.

Obviously these kids' parents, like mine, encouraged their reading. Except that their parents, unlike mine, knew *where* and *how* to direct their children's reading. But if academic intelligence is, as I do believe, largely a matter of cultural background, I was soon to discover that I too had an advantage over most of my peers. From the regular intelligence tests that they used to give us, I came to understand that these students were no smarter than I.

I have no idea what these tests are like today. But when I was in high school, they consisted of three parts: vocabulary, reading comprehension, and math. And whenever we would take these tests, I'd whup the class. I mean, I'd whup 'em hands down. It's hard to say who was the more surprised, me or them. These were disciplined students with strong intellectual backgrounds who were *very* competitive. Yet, I was beating them?

By about my junior year I figured out the source of my advantage: my uncle Lew.

Within the family, the authority on things academic was Uncle Lew, my mother's uncle. Dr. Lewellyn Silcote was a physician educated at City College and Meharry Medical College in Nashville. Whenever he came to visit, we discussed my education and my prospects. Remember the only three avenues to economic independence thought available to African men then? Well, whenever we'd talk, I'd say, "I'm thinking about being a doctor like you." Uncle Lew would say, "In that case, study Latin. A lot of medical and anatomical terminology is based on Latin."

"What if I'm a lawyer?"

"Same thing. Just about all legal terms are in Latin."

"And if I decide to be a preacher?"

"There too, Latin again."

So I studied Latin and continued to do so all the time at Science. I studied Latin for four years. I read Cicero in Latin. I read Caesar in Latin. And of course Latin has a vast vocabulary. More important, this is the vocabulary from which much of the English vocabulary has evolved. Most of my peers at Science were studying French, which, relative to Latin and English, has a much smaller vocabulary.

So even were I a C student in Latin while you were an A student in French, if we took a vocabulary test, I should whup you, hands down. And since reading comprehension is based on vocabulary and recognition of usage and syntax, my wide if unselective reading was useful there. So I always dominated those two sections while also holding my own in math since it was logical and most times you could check your answers. . . .

The Science experience over the next four years could not fail to have a profound effect on me in many, many ways.

Academically it was rigorous, completely a product of the Western Enlightenment: reason and the scientific method. The curriculum and approach were heavily focused on Western rationalism, scientific materialism, the physical sciences, and the scientific method, all of which I found logical and thus intellectually satisfying. This empiricism was as suited to the medical studies I then projected as to the study of social history and revolutionary theory and practice. Now the political would touch on the academic. . . .

One of the great political and cultural resources for me at this time was Michaux's famous African Bookstore on 125th Street, which I would visit every chance I got. Mr. Michaux saw that I liked to read about our people and took an interest in me. One day I asked Mr. Michaux about Padmore. He showed me a copy of Padmore's *Pan-Africanism or Communism* and explained that Padmore was a great Pan-Africanist thinker who was an adviser or mentor to Kwame Nkrumah. I was fascinated. I did not have the money at the time to buy the book but I skimmed through it eagerly. Later I would study Padmore and become one of his greatest supporters. Even today I always refer to Padmore as a seminal Pan-Africanist and encourage all Pan-Africanists to study and learn from him.

Later I learned with interest that Padmore was born in Trinidad—he died in Africa—and that his original family name was Seymour Nurse. Nurse is a prominent name in the African community in Trinidad. I also learned that during his boyhood in Belmont (close to where my father had built his house), one of his playmates was young Cyril James.

Whenever C. L. R. James's name came up among the white leftists I knew in high school, he was more or less pigeonholed as a "Trotskyite," hence a revisionist and apostate from the "correct" line. But to the speakers on 125th Street, C. L. R. James was an African revolutionary thinker. Later when I came to read his *Black Jacobins*, I was thrilled—moved and inspired. That book is a powerful historical classic on the revolutionary struggle against slavery in Haiti, which especially emphasizes the revolutionary roles, spirit, and character of Haiti's African masses in that struggle. I was just overwhelmed. I loved it. I strongly recommend this great book to young Africans interested in their peoples' legacy of struggle.

Still later I would discover another of Harlem's great treasures, the Schomburg Collection. When Malcolm X began to become a presence in Harlem as the dynamic young minister who was organizing Mohammed's Mosque #7, a story began to circulate that established the young minster's character.

According to the story, Malcolm was driving along and saw a group of young brothers shooting craps on a sidewalk. He stopped the car and approached the game. He either seized or put his foot on the dice. Of course, the players started to get into they bad bags. Malcolm froze them with that look he had. My young brothers, you know what this building is? he asked. Yeah, I thought so. You don't know, do you? This is the Schomburg Collection. It's got damn near everything ever written by or about black people. And what you doing? Instead of being inside learning about yourself, your people, and our history, you out here in darkness shooting dice. That's what's wrong with us, why Mr. Muhammad says, "If you want to hide something from the black man, put it in a library."

Now, I was not among those crapshooters. But the story impressed on me the importance of the Schomburg and I began to spend many a profitable hour there. . . .

Early in my senior year the Young Communists at Science organized a bus for a demonstration against the House Un-American Activities Committee in Washington. I was on the bus. I am not sure whether I was the sole African on that bus, but if I wasn't we sure were not many. This would not have been unusual in left political actions at Science, so I never gave it a thought.

The demonstration was in progress (I think at the White House, but it could have been the Capitol—official Washington, anyway) when our bus pulled up. We streamed off and approached the picket line, which was of impressive size given the oppressive political climate in the country at the time. As we approached the pickets, I saw something that would profoundly affect the direction of my life.

A section of the line was black. The marchers were not only all African, but they were all about my age. Man, I jes' rushed over.

"Hey, y'all. Who are you guys with? The Young Socialists? The Communists?"

"No, man. We're NAG," said a brother who introduced himself later as John Moody.

"Yeah? And what's NAG, my man?"

"That's the Nonviolent Action Group from Howard University. Whyn't you join us?"

I jumped on the line and the brothers and sisters told me about Howard and NAG. That they were affiliated with the Student Nonviolent Coordinating Committee (SNCC). That they had been campaigning in Virginia and Maryland and in D.C., the nation's capital. They struck me as smart, serious, political, sassy—and they were black.

All the way back to New York I was intensely excited. I was surprised at how excited I'd become to discover young Africans who were committed activists. But I was pretty certain that I'd solved the college question.

Everything I later found out about Howard confirmed the fit: Howard was a historic black school founded during Reconstruction to educate the children of "the freedmen." It was named for its first president, General Oliver Otis Howard, a Union general and abolitionist. More to the point, its medical school was said to have produced a majority of the doctors in the African community here and abroad.

In my mind, the choice of college had been a done deal from the conversations on that picket line at the White House. When we'd left, I'd said, "I'll see you in September." And while I would apply to and enroll at Howard University, it was NAG I was really joining.

But at first my parents weren't sure.

According to my mother, "During his last year in high school, Stokely started talking about Howard University. His father and I figured, because everyone said he was so smart, that he should go to Harvard. But every time we said 'Harvard,' he said 'Howard.' It was 'Harvard.' 'No, Howard.' Until finally we put the case to my uncle Lew, the psychiatrist, who was the family authority on all things educational."

Dr. Silcote's advice carried the day. He said that beyond a certain point the student was more important than the school. A serious student could get an excellent education at either place, as good an education at Howard as at Harvard. Besides which, he said, the friends you make in college tend to be friends for life. So Howard it was to be. Besides, it sure was a lot more affordable.

Twenty-One

ALICE WALKER

*Writing poems is my way of celebrating with the world
that I have not committed suicide the evening before.*

Alice Walker was born in 1944 in Eatonton, Georgia, and lives in Northern California. An internationally celebrated writer, poet, and activist, she created the term "womanist" to define Black feminism.

Her bestselling books include numerous novels, collections of essays and short stories, children's books, and volumes of poetry. In 1983, for her novel *The Color Purple*, Walker made history as the first African American woman to win a Pulitzer Prize for Fiction. That same year she won the National Book Award. *The Color Purple* also became an Academy Award–nominated film in 1985 and was adapted for the Broadway stage and won a Tony Award in 2006. The author continues to write prolifically, including a blog on her official website, AliceWalkersGarden.com.

In this excerpt from her book *In Search of Our Mothers' Gardens: Womanist Prose*, Walker shares a personal and dark time of her last year of college, in which writing poetry brought her back to life and light.

have always been a solitary person, and since I was eight years old (and victim of a traumatic accident that blinded and scarred one eye), I have daydreamed—not of fairy tales—but of falling on swords, of putting guns to my heart or head, and of slashing my wrists with a razor. For a long time I thought I was very ugly and disfigured. This made me shy and timid, and I often reacted to insults and slights that were not intended. I discovered the cruelty (legendary) of children, and of relatives, and could not recognize it as the curiosity it was.

I believe, though, that it was from this period—from my solitary, lonely position, the position of an outcast—that I began really to see people and things, really to notice relationships and to learn to be patient enough to care about how they turned out. I no longer felt like the little girl I was. I felt old, and because I felt I was unpleasant to look at, filled with shame. I retreated into solitude, and read stories and began to write poems.

But it was not until my last year in college that I realized, nearly, the consequences of my daydreams. That year I made myself acquainted with every philosopher's position on suicide, because by that time it did not seem frightening or even odd—but only inevitable. Nietzsche and Camus made the most sense, and were neither maudlin nor pious. God's displeasure didn't seem to matter much to them, and I had reached the same conclusion. But in addition to finding such dispassionate commentary from them—although both hinted at the cowardice involved, and that bothered me—I had been to Africa during the summer, and returned to school healthy and brown, and loaded down with sculptures and orange fabric—and pregnant.

I felt at the mercy of everything, including my own body, which I had learned to accept as a kind of casing over what I considered my real self. As long as it functioned properly I dressed it, pampered it, led it into acceptable arms, and forgot about it. But now it refused to function properly. I was so sick I could not even bear the smell of fresh air. And I had no money, and I was, essentially—as I had been since grade school—alone. I felt there was no way out, and I was not romantic enough to believe in maternal instincts alone as a means of survival; in any case, I did not seem to possess those instincts. But I knew no one who knew about the secret, scary thing abortion was. And so, when all my efforts at finding an abortionist failed, I planned to kill myself, or—as I thought of it then—to "give myself a little rest." I stopped going down the hill to meals because I vomited incessantly, even when nothing came up but yellow, bitter bile. I lay on my bed in a cold sweat, my head spinning.

While I was lying there, I thought of my mother, to whom abortion is a sin; her face appeared framed in the window across from me, her head wreathed in sunflowers and giant elephant-ears (my mother's flowers love her; they grow as tall as she wants); I thought of my father, that suspecting, once-fat, slowly shrinking man, who had not helped me at all since I was twelve years old, when he bought me a pair of ugly saddle oxfords I refused to wear. I thought of my sisters, who had their own problems (when approached with the problem I had, one sister never replied, the other told me—in forty-five minutes of long-distance carefully enunciated language— that I was a slut). I thought of the people at my high-school gradua- tion who had managed to collect seventy-five dollars, to send me to college. I thought of my sister's check for a hundred dollars that she gave me for finishing high school at the head of my class: a check I never cashed, because I knew it would bounce.

I think it was at this point that I allowed myself exactly two self-pitying tears; I had wasted so much, how dared I? But I hated myself for crying, so I stopped, comforted by knowing I would not have to cry—or see anyone else cry—again.

I did not eat or sleep for three days. My mind refused, at times, to think about my problem at all—it jumped ahead to the solution. I prayed to—but I don't know Who or What I prayed to, or even if I did. Perhaps I prayed to God a while, and then to the Great Void a while. When I thought of my family, and when—on the third day—I began to see their faces around the walls, I realized they would be shocked and hurt to learn of my death, but I felt they would not care deeply at all, when they discovered I was pregnant. Essentially, they would believe I was evil. They would be ashamed of me.

For three days I lay on the bed with a razor blade under my pillow. My secret was known to three friends only—all inexperienced (except verbally), and helpless. They came often to cheer me up, to bring me up to date on things as frivolous as classes. I was touched by their kindness, and loved them. But each time they left, I took out my razor blade and pressed it deep into my arm. I practiced a slicing motion. So that when there was no longer any hope, I would be able to cut my wrists quickly, and (I hoped) painlessly.

In those three days, I said good-bye to the world (this seemed like a high-flown sentiment, even then, but everything was beginning to be unreal); I realized how much I loved it, and how hard it would be not to see the sunrise every morning, the snow, the sky, the trees, the rocks, the faces of people, all so different (and it was during this period that all things began to flow together; the face of one of my friends revealed itself to be the friendly, gentle face of a lion, and I asked her one day if I could touch her face and stroke her mane. I felt her face and hair, and she really was a lion; I began to feel the possibility of someone as worthless as myself attaining wisdom). But I found, as I had found on the porch of a building in Liberty County, Georgia—when rocks and bottles bounced off me as I sat looking up at the stars—that I was not afraid of death. In a way, I began looking forward to it. I felt tired. Most of the poems on suicide in *Once* come from my feelings during this period of waiting.

On the last day for miracles, one of my friends telephoned to say someone had given her a telephone number. I called from school, hoping for nothing, and made an appointment. I went to see the doctor and he put me to sleep. When I woke up, my friend was standing over me holding a red rose. She was a blonde, gray-eyed girl, who loved horses and tennis, and she said nothing as she handed me back my life. That moment is engraved on my mind—her smile, sad and pained and frightfully young—as she tried so hard to stand by me and be my friend. She drove me back to school and tucked me in. My other friend, brown, a wisp of blue and scarlet, with hair like thunder, brought me food.

That week I wrote without stopping (except to eat and go to the toilet) almost all of the poems in *Once*—with the exception of one or two, perhaps, and these I do not remember.

I wrote them all in a tiny blue notebook that I can no longer find—the African ones first, because the vitality and color and friendships in Africa rushed over me in dreams the first night I slept. I had not thought about Africa (except to talk about it) since I returned. All the sculptures and weavings I had given away, because they seemed to emit an odor that made me more nauseated than the smell of fresh air. Then I wrote the suicide poems, because I felt I understood the part played in suicide by circumstances and fatigue. I also began to understand how alone woman is, because of her body. Then I wrote the love poems (love real and love imagined), and tried to reconcile myself to all things human. "Johann" is the most extreme example of this need to love even the most unfamiliar, the most fearful. For, actually, when I traveled in Germany I was in a constant state of terror, and no amount of flattery from handsome young German men could shake it. Then I wrote the poems of struggle in the South. The picketing, the marching, all the things that had been buried, because when I thought about them the pain caused a paralysis of intellectual and moral confusion. The anger and humiliation I had suffered were always in conflict with the elation, the exaltation, the *joy* I felt when I could leave each vicious encounter or confrontation whole, and not—like the people before me—spewing obscenities or throwing bricks. For, during those encounters, I had begun to comprehend what it meant to be lost.

Each morning, the poems finished during the night were stuffed under Muriel Rukeyser's door—her classroom was an old gardener's cottage in the middle of the campus. Then I would hurry back to my room to write some more. I didn't care what she did with the poems. I only knew I wanted someone to read them as if they were new leaves sprouting from an old tree. The same energy that impelled me to write them carried them to her door.

This was the winter of 1965, and my last three months in college. I was twenty-one years old, although *Once* was not published till three years later, when I was twenty-four. (Muriel Rukeyser gave the poems to her agent, who gave them to Hiram Haydn at Harcourt Brace Jovanovich—who said right away that he wanted them; so I cannot claim to have had a hard time publishing, yet.) By the time *Once* was published, it no longer seemed important—I was surprised when it went, almost immediately, into a second printing—that is, the book itself did not seem to me important; only the writing of the poems, which clarified for me how very much I loved being alive. It was this feeling of gladness that carried over into my first published short story, "To Hell with Dying," about an old man saved from death countless times by the love of his neighbor's children. I was the children, and the old man.

I have gone into this memory because I think it might be important for other women to share. I don't enjoy contemplating it; I wish it had never happened. But if it had not, I firmly believe I would never have survived to be a writer. I know I would not have survived at all.

Since that time, it seems to me that all of my poems—and I write groups of poems rather than singles—are written when I have successfully pulled myself out of a completely numbing despair, and stand again in the sunlight. Writing poems is my way of celebrating with the world that I have not committed suicide the evening before.

Langston Hughes wrote in his autobiography that when he was sad, he wrote his best poems. When he was happy, he didn't write anything. This is true of me, where poems are concerned. When I am happy (or neither happy nor sad), I write essays, short stories, and novels. Poems—even happy ones—emerge from an accumulation of sadness. . . .

————

The writing of my poetry is never consciously planned; although I become aware that there are certain emotions I would like to explore. Perhaps my unconscious begins working on poems from these emotions long before I am aware of it. I have learned to wait patiently (sometimes refusing good lines, images, when they come to me, for fear they are not lasting), until a poem is ready to present itself—*all* of itself, if possible. I sometimes feel the urge to write poems way in advance of ever sitting down to write. There is a definite restlessness, a kind of feverish excitement that is tinged with dread. The dread is because after writing each batch of poems I am always convinced that I will never write poems again. I become aware that I am controlled by them, not the other way around. I put off writing as long as I can. Then I lock myself in my study, write lines and lines and lines, then put them away, underneath other papers, without looking at them for a long time. I am afraid that if I read them too soon they will turn into trash, or, worse, something so topical and transient as to have no meaning—not even to me—after a few weeks. (This is how my later poetry-writing differs from the way I wrote *Once.*) I also attempt, in this way, to guard against the human tendency to try to make poetry carry the weight of half-truths, of cleverness. I realize that while I am writing poetry, I am so high as to feel invisible, and in that condition it is possible to write anything.

A Temporary Library in a Small Place

JAMAICA KINCAID

Why, years after The Earthquake damaged the
old library building, has a new library not been
built? Why is the library above a dry-goods store
in an old run-down cement-brick building?

Jamaica Kincaid was born in 1949 in Antigua. Named Elaine Potter
Richardson, she changed her name once she settled in New York City
and began to write short fiction. A novelist and essayist, Kincaid has
been published in the *Village Voice* and the *Paris Review*, among others.
The *New Yorker* published excerpts of her novels *Annie John*, about a
mother-daughter relationship set in Antigua, and *Lucy*, which created a
publishing sensation as the plot seemed to follow her own experience of
being brought to the United States as an au pair and having an antag-
onistic relationship with her White, wealthy employers. Kincaid spent
twenty years at the *New Yorker* as a staff writer before becoming a professor of literature, first at Harvard University, and currently at Claremont
McKenna College.

A *Small Place*, published in 1988, is Kincaid's nonfictional depic-
tion of colonial life in Antigua before the country's independence in
1981. Here, in a passage from that book, Kincaid laments the loss in an
earthquake of the public library that meant so much to her childhood.

You can imagine how I felt when, one day, in Antigua, standing on Market Street, looking up one way and down the other, I asked myself: Is the Antigua I see before me, self-ruled, a worse place than what it was when it was dominated by the bad-minded English and all the bad-minded things they brought with them? How did Antigua get to such a state that I would have to ask myself this? For the answer on every Antiguan's lips to the question "What is going on here now?" is "The government is corrupt. Them are thief, them are big thief." Imagine, then, the bitterness and the shame in me as I tell you this. I was standing on Market Street in front of the library. The library! But why is the library on Market Street? I had asked myself. Why is the old building that was damaged in the famous earthquake years ago, the building that has the legend on it THIS BUILDING WAS DAMAGED IN THE EARTHQUAKE OF 1974. REPAIRS ARE PENDING, not repaired and the library put back in the place where it used to be? Or, why, years after The Earthquake damaged the old library building, has a new library not been built? Why is the library above a dry-goods store in an old run-down cement-brick building? Oh, you might be saying to yourself, Why is she so undone at what has become of the library, why does she think that is a good example of corruption, of things gone bad? But if you saw the old library, situated as it was, in a big, old wooden building painted a shade of yellow that is beautiful to people like me, with its wide veranda, its big, always open windows, its rows and rows of shelves filled with books, its beautiful wooden tables and chairs for sitting and reading, if you could hear the sound of its quietness (for the quiet in this library was a sound in itself), the smell of the sea (which was a stone's throw away), the heat of the sun (no building could protect us from that), the beauty of us sitting there like communicants at an altar, taking in, again and again, the fairy tale of how we met you, your right to do the things you did, how beautiful you were, are, and always will be; if you could see all of that in just one glimpse, you would see why my heart would break at the dung heap that now passes for a library in Antigua. The place where the library is now, above the dry-goods store, in the old run-down concrete building, is too small to hold all the books from the old building, and so most of the books, instead of being on their nice shelves, resting comfortably, waiting to acquaint me with you in all your greatness, are in cardboard boxes in a room, gathering mildew, or dust, or ruin. In this place, the young librarians cannot find the things they want and I don't know whether it is because of the chaos of storing for a long period of time the contents of a public library in cardboard boxes, or because of the bad post-colonial education the young librarians have received. (In Antigua today, most young people seem almost illiterate. On the airwaves, where they work as news personalities, they speak English as if it were their sixth language. Once, I attended an event at carnival time called a "Teenage Pageant." In this event, teenagers, male and female, paraded around on a stadium stage, singing pop songs—a hideous song called "The Greatest Love" was a particular favourite among them to perform—reciting poems they had written about slavery—there is an appropriate obsession with slavery—and generally making asses of themselves. What surprised me most about them was not how familiar they were with the rubbish of North America—compared to the young people of my generation, who were familiar with the rubbish of England—but, unlike my generation, how stupid they seemed, how unable they were to answer in a straightforward way, and in their native tongue of English, simple questions about themselves. In my generation they would not have been allowed on the school stage, much less before an audience in a stadium.) The head librarian, the same one from colonial days, seemed to spend her time wondering if there was anybody with money or influence to help the library, apologizing to people—Antiguans returning to Antigua after a long absence—who are shocked and offended by the sight of the library sitting on top of a dry-goods store, wondering if in the end the people at the Mill Reef Club will relent and contribute their money to the building of a new library, instead of holding to their repair-of-the-old-library-or-nothing position. (The people at the Mill Reef

Club love the old Antigua. I love the old Antigua. Without question, we don't have the same old Antigua in mind.) When I was growing up and was a member of the library, this woman was the head librarian. In those days, she seemed imperious and stuck-up, suspicious of us (in my case, she was justified; I stole many books from this library. I didn't mean to steal the books, really; it's just that once I had read a book I couldn't bear to part with it), always sure that we meant to do some bad. She must have been very proud of her work then and her association with such an institution, for, to see her now, she looks the opposite of her old self. I would go to that library every Saturday afternoon—the last stop on my Saturday-afternoon round of things to do (I would save this for last, for it was the thing I liked to do best)—and sit and look at books and think about the misery in being me (I was a child and what is a child if not someone full of herself or himself), whom I loved, whom I did not love, whom I only just liked, and so on. I think that by around nine years of age I had read all the books in the children's section (it was a very small collection), and so I had to use my mother's library card to borrow books from the adult section. It is this same librarian who now stands over the shame of what is now the library who used to watch me closely, trying to make sure that I didn't leave the library with more books than I was allowed, and leave with them in such a way that meant they would never be seen in any library but my own again. This woman kept a close watch on me, making sure that I didn't walk out with books held tightly between my legs (what a trick, I thought) or in the basket that I carried to hold my Saturday-afternoon purchases. And so again, can you see why it is that the library might mean something to me, why it might make me feel sad to see it reduced to its present condition? For at the moment that I was standing on Market Street and looking up at the thing called the library, the old building where the library used to be was occupied by, and served as headquarters for, a carnival troupe. The theme of this carnival troupe was "Angels from the Realm," and it seemed to me that there was something in that, though not a deliberate something, just a something, like an "Angels from the Realm of Innocence" something. (And I supposed it made sense for something from the realm of culture to occupy a building that used to house something from the realm of education, for in Antigua, the Minister of Education is also the Minister of Culture.) Where the shelves of books used to be, where the wooden tables and chairs used to be, where the sound of quietness used to be, where the smell of the sea used to be, where everything used to be, was now occupied by costumes: costumes for angels from the realm. Some of the costumes were for angels before the Fall, some of the costumes were for angels after the Fall; the ones representing After the Fall were the best. And so what sort of place has Antigua become that the people from the Mill Reef Club are allowed a say in anything? That they are allowed to live there the way they continue to live there is bad enough. I then went to see a woman whose family had helped to establish the Mill Reef Club. She had been mentioned to me as someone who was very active in getting the old library restored. I knew of this woman, for she is notorious for liking Antiguans only if they are servants. After I mentioned the library to her, the first thing she told me was that she always encouraged her girls and her girls' children to use the library, and by her girls she meant grownup Antiguan women (not unlike me) who work in her gift shop as seamstresses and saleswomen. She said to me then what everybody in Antigua says sooner or later: The government is for sale; anybody from anywhere can come to Antigua and for a sum of money can get what he wants. And I had to ask myself, What exactly should I feel toward the people who robbed me of the right to make a reply to this woman? For I could see the pleasure she took in pointing out to me the gutter into which a self-governing—black—Antigua had placed itself. In any case, this woman and her friends at the Mill Reef Club wanted to restore the old library, but she said she didn't know if they would be able to do so, because that part of St. John's was going to be developed, turned into little shops—boutiques—so that when tourists turned up they could buy all those awful things that tourists always buy, all those awful things they then take home, put in their attics, and their children have to throw out when the tour-

ists, finally, die. I had heard from many people that the person who
wanted to develop that part of St. John's was a foreigner, who was
once wanted in the Far East for swindling a government out of oil
profits, a man so notorious that he cannot travel with a passport
from the country of which he is a citizen but travels on a diplomatic
passport issued by the government of Antigua. I thought, then, that
I should ask the Minister of Education about the library. I am sure
he would have had a good explanation for why it is that for so many
years this island, which has as its motto of Independence "A People
to Mold, A Nation to Build" has not had a proper library, but at the
moment that I wanted to ask him this question he was in Trinidad
attending a cricket match, something he must have been bound to
do, since he is not only the Minister of Education and the Minister
of Culture but also the Minister of Sport. In Antigua, cricket is sport
and cricket is culture. (But let me just tell you something about
Ministers of Culture: in places where there is a Minister of Culture
it means there is no culture. For have you ever heard of any culture
springing up under the umbrella of a Minister of Culture? Countries
with Minsters of Culture must be like countries with Liberty Weekend. Do you remember Liberty Weekend? In the week before Liberty Weekend, the United States Supreme Court ruled that ordinary
grown-up people could not do as they pleased behind the locked
doors of their own bedroom. I would have thought, then, that the
people whose idea it was to have the Liberty Weekend business
would have been so ashamed at such a repudiation of liberty that
they would have cancelled the whole thing. But not at all; and so in
a country that had less liberty than it used to have, Liberty Weekend
was celebrated. In countries that have no culture or are afraid they
may have no culture, there is a Minister of Culture. And what is
culture, anyway? In some places, it's the way they play drums; in
other places, it's the way you behave out in public; and in still other
places, it's just the way a person cooks food. And so what is there to
preserve about these things? For is it not so that people make them
up as they go along, make them up as they need them?) Oh, I suppose that it was just as well that the Minister of Culture was not in

Antigua then, for I did not know how this man would take to me or anything that I might say.

———

EDITOR'S NOTE: *In 1974, the national public library of Antigua and Barbuda was destroyed by an earthquake. After forty years of operating in a temporary space on Market Street, in April of 2014, the library's permanent home moved to a 20,000 square-foot multilevel building on Hailes Promenade. According to the government's website, at the ribbon-cutting ceremony Dr. Hon. Jacqui Quinn-Leandro, the fifth education minister to preside over the library construction project, stated, "Any Antiguan and Barbudan forty years or younger would not have known or had the benefit of a properly well-run, well-resourced national public library. And I say without equivocation this is a burning shame, a disgrace, and a national travesty. However, today is a historic day."*

What Is an African American Classic?

HENRY LOUIS GATES JR.

The quest for freedom and literacy—the literacy of
great literature—are inextricably intertwined.

Henry Louis Gates Jr. is the Alphonse Fletcher University Professor and
director of the W. E. B. Du Bois Institute for African and African American Research at Harvard University. Born in 1950 in West Virginia, Gates
is the editor in chief of the news and culture website TheRoot.com and
host of *Finding Your Roots* on PBS.

The author and editor of many books, including his 1994 memoir,
Colored People, he is general editor for the Penguin Classics series of
African American works, such as *Twelve Years a Slave*, in which the following piece on what forms the canon of classic books by African American authors was published as an introductory essay. In it, he says he has
tried to be "an evangelist" for literature written by Black authors. I have
long admired Gates's work in unearthing and republishing lost writings
of African Americans, such as his 1981 rediscovery of *Our Nig: Sketches
from the Life of a Free Black* by Harriet E. Wilson, which is considered
the first novel published (in 1859) by a Black woman in North America.

have long nurtured a deep and abiding affection for the Penguin Classics, at least since I was an undergraduate at Yale. I used to imagine that my attraction for these books—grouped together, as a set, in some independent bookstores when I was a student, and perhaps even in some today—stemmed from the fact that my first-grade classmates, for some reason that I can't recall, were required to dress as penguins in our annual all-school pageant, and perform a collective side-to-side motion that our misguided teacher thought she could choreograph into something meant to pass for a "dance." Piedmont, West Virginia, in 1956, was a very long way from Penguin Nation, wherever that was supposed to be! But penguins we were determined to be, and we did our level best to avoid wounding each other with our orange-colored cardboard beaks while stomping out of rhythm in our matching orange, veined webbed feet. The whole scene was madness, one never to be repeated at the Davis Free School. But I never stopped loving the penguins. And I have never stopped loving the very audacity of the idea of the Penguin Classics, an affordable, accessible library of the most important and compelling texts in the history of civilization, their black-and-white spines and covers and uniform type giving each text a comfortable, familiar feel, as if we have encountered it, or its cousins, before. I think of the Penguin Classics as the very best and most compelling in human thought, an Alexandrian library in paperback, enclosed in black and white.

I still gravitate to the Penguin Classics when killing time in an airport bookstore, deferring the slow torture of the security lines. Sometimes I even purchase two or three, fantasizing that I can speed-read one of the shorter titles, then make a dent in the longer one, vainly attempting to fill the holes in the liberal arts education that our degrees suggest we have, over the course of a plane ride! Mark Twain once quipped that a classic is "something that everybody wants to have read and nobody wants to read," and perhaps that applies to my airport purchasing habits. For my generation, these titles in the Penguin Classics form the canon—the canon of the texts that a truly well-educated person should have read, and read carefully and closely, at least once. For years I rued the absence of texts by black authors in this series, and longed to be able to make even a small contribution to the diversification of this astonishingly universal list. I watched with great pleasure as titles by African American and African authors began to appear, some two dozen over the past several years. So when Elda Rotor approached me about editing a series of African American classics and collections for Penguin's Portable Series, I eagerly accepted.

Thinking about the titles appropriate for inclusion in these series led me, inevitably, to think about what, for me, constitutes a "classic." And thinking about this led me, in turn, to the wealth of reflections on what defines a work of literature or philosophy somehow speaking to the human condition beyond time and place, a work somehow endlessly compelling, generation upon generation, a work whose author we don't have to look like to identify with, to feel at one with, as we find ourselves transported through the magic of a textual time machine; a work that refracts the image of ourselves that we project onto it, regardless of our ethnicity, our gender, our time, our place. This is what centuries of scholars and writers have meant when they use the word "classic," and—despite all that we know about the complex intersubjectivity of the production of meaning in the wondrous exchange between a reader and text—it remains true that classic texts, even in the most conventional, conservative sense of the word "classic," do exist, and these books will continue to be read long after the generation the text reflects and defines, the generation of readers contemporary with the text's author, is dead and gone. Classic texts speak from their authors' graves, in their names, in their voices. As Italo Calvino once remarked, "A classic is a book that has never finished saying what it has to say."

Faulkner put this idea in an interesting way: "The aim of every artist is to arrest motion, which is life, by artificial means, and hold it fixed so that a hundred years later, when a stranger looks at it, it moves again since it is life." That, I am certain, must be the desire of every writer. But what about the reader? What makes a book a classic to a reader? Here, perhaps, Hemingway said it best: "All good books are alike in that they are truer than if they had really happened and after you are finished reading one you will feel that all that happened to you, and afterwards it belongs to you, the good and the bad, the ecstasy, the remorse and sorrow, the people and the places and how the weather was."

I have been reading black literature since I was fifteen, yanked into the dark discursive universe by an Episcopal priest at a church camp near my home in West Virginia in August of 1965, during the terrifying days of the Watts Riots in Los Angeles. Eventually, by fits and starts, studying the literature written by black authors became my avocation; ultimately it has become my vocation. And, in my own way, I have tried to be an evangelist for it, to a readership larger than my own people, people who, as it were, look like these texts. Here, I am reminded of something W. S. Merwin said about the books he most loved: "Perhaps a classic is a work that one imagines should be common knowledge, but more and more often isn't." I would say, of African and African American literature, that perhaps classic works by black writers are works that one imagines should be common knowledge among the broadest possible readership but that less and less are, as the teaching of reading to understand how words can create the worlds into which books can transport us yields to classroom instruction geared toward passing a state-authorized, standardized exam. All literary texts suffer from this wrongheaded approach to teaching, mind you; but it especially affects texts by people of color, and texts by women—texts still struggling, despite enormous gains over the last twenty years, to gain a solid foothold in anthologies and syllabi. For every anthology, every syllabus, every publishing series such as the Penguin Classics constitutes a distinct "canon," an implicit definition of all that is essential for a truly educated person to read.

James Baldwin, who has pride of place in my personal canon of African American authors since it was one of his books that the Episcopal priest gave me to read in that dreadful summer of 1965, argued that "the responsibility of a writer is to excavate the experience of the people who produced him." But surely Baldwin would have agreed with E. M. Forster that the books that we remember, the books that have truly influenced us, are those that "have gone a little further down our particular path than we have yet ourselves." Excavating the known is a worthy goal of the writer as cultural archaeologist; yet, at the same time, so is unveiling the unknown, the unarticulated yet shared experience of the colorless things that make us human: "something we have always known (or thought we knew)," as Calvino puts it, "but without knowing that this author said it first." We might think of the difference between Forster and Baldwin, on the one hand, and Calvino, on the other, as the difference between an author representing what has happened (Forster, Baldwin) in the history of a people whose stories, whose very history itself, has long been suppressed, and what could have happened (Calvino) in the atemporal realm of art. This is an important distinction when thinking about the nature of an African American classic—rather, when thinking about the nature of the texts that comprise the African American literary tradition or, for that matter, the texts in any under-read tradition.

One of James Baldwin's most memorable essays, a subtle meditation on sexual preference, race, and gender, is entitled "Here Be Dragons." So much of traditional African American literature, even fiction and poetry—ostensibly at least once removed from direct statement—was meant to deal a fatal blow to the dragon of racism. For black writers since the eighteenth-century beginnings of the tradition, literature has been one more weapon—a very important weapon, mind you, but still one weapon among many—in the arsenal black people have drawn upon to fight against antiblack racism and for their equal rights before the law. Ted Joans, the black surrealist poet, called this sort of literature from the sixties' Black Art movement "hand grenade poems." Of what possible use are the niceties of figuration when one must slay a dragon? I can hear you say give me the blunt weapon anytime! Problem is, it is more difficult than some writers seem to think to slay a dragon with a poem or a novel.

Social problems persist; literature too tied to addressing those social problems tends to enter the historical archives, leaving the realm of the literary. Let me state bluntly what should be obvious: writers are read for how they write, not what they write about.

Frederick Douglass—for this generation of readers one of the most widely read writers—reflected on this matter even in the midst of one of his most fiery speeches addressing the ironies of the sons and daughters of slaves celebrating the Fourth of July while slavery continued unabated. In his now-classic essay "What Is to the Slave the Fourth of July" (1852), Douglass argued that an immediate, almost transparent form of discourse was demanded of black writers by the heated temper of the times, a discourse with an immediate end in mind: "At a time like this, scorching irony, not convincing argument, is needed. . . . a fiery stream of biting ridicule, blasting reproach, withering sarcasm, and stern rebuke. For it is not light that is needed, but fire; it is not the gentle shower, but thunder. We need the storm, the whirlwind, and the earthquake." Above all else, Douglass concludes, the rhetoric of the literature created by African Americans must, of necessity, be a purposeful rhetoric, its ends targeted at attacking the evils that afflict black people: "The feeling of the nation must be quickened; the conscience of the nation must be roused; the propriety of the nation must be startled; the hypocrisy of the nation must be exposed; and its crimes against God and man must be proclaimed and denounced." And perhaps this was so; nevertheless, we read Douglass's writings today in literature classes not so much for their content but to understand, and marvel at, his sublime mastery of words, words—to paraphrase Calvino—that never finish saying what it is they have to say, not because of their "message," but because of the language in which that message is inextricably enfolded.

There are as many ways to define a classic in the African American tradition as there are in any other tradition, and these ways are legion. So many essays have been published entitled "What Is a Classic?" that they could fill several large anthologies. And while no one can say explicitly why generations of readers return to read certain texts, just about everyone can agree that making a best-seller list in one's lifetime is most certainly not an index of fame or influence over time; the longevity of one's readership—of books about which one says, "I am rereading," as Calvino puts it—on the other hand, most certainly is. So, the size of one's readership (through library use, Internet access, and sales) cumulatively is an interesting factor to consider; and because of series such as the Penguin Classics, we can gain a sense, for our purposes, of those texts written by authors in previous generations that have sustained sales—mostly for classroom use—long after their authors were dead.

There can be little doubt that *Narrative of the Life of Frederick Douglass* (1845), *The Souls of Black Folks* (1903), by W. E. B. Du Bois, and *Their Eyes Were Watching God* (1937), by Zora Neale Hurston, are the three most classic of the black classics—again, as measured by consumption—while Langston Hughes's poetry, though not purchased as books in these large numbers, is accessed through the Internet as frequently as that of any other American poet, and indeed profoundly more so than most. Within Penguin's Portable Series list, the most popular individual titles, excluding Douglass's first slave narrative and Du Bois's *Souls*, are:

Up from Slavery (1903), Booker T. Washington
The Autobiography of an Ex-Coloured Man (1912), James
    Weldon Johnson
God's Trombones (1926), James Weldon Johnson
Passing (1929), Nella Larsen
The Marrow of Tradition (1898), Charles W. Chesnutt
Incidents in the Life of a Slave Girl (1861), Harriet Jacobs
The Interesting Narrative (1789), Olaudah Equiano
The House Behind the Cedars (1900), Charles W. Chesnutt
My Bondage and My Freedom (1855), Frederick Douglass
Quicksand (1928), Nella Larsen

These titles form a canon of classics of African American literature, judged by classroom readership. If we add Jean Toomer's novel

Cane (1922), arguably the first work of African American modernism, along with Douglass's first narrative, Du Bois's *The Souls*, and Hurston's *Their Eyes*, we would most certainly have included many of the touchstones of black literature published before 1940, when Richard Wright published *Native Son*.

Every teacher's syllabus constitutes a canon of sorts, and I teach these texts and a few others as the classics of the black canon. Why these particular texts? I can think of two reasons: First, these texts signify or riff upon each other, repeating, borrowing, and extending metaphors book to book, generation to generation. To take just a few examples, Equiano's eighteenth-century use of the trope of the talking book (an image found, remarkably, in five slave narratives published between 1770 and 1811) becomes, with Frederick Douglass, the representation of the quest for freedom as, necessarily, the quest for literacy, for a freedom larger than physical manumission; we might think of this as the representation of metaphysical manumission, of freedom and literacy—the literacy of great literature— inextricably intertwined. Douglass transformed the metaphor of the talking book into the trope of chiasmus, a repetition with a stinging reversal: "You have seen how a man becomes a slave, you will see how a slave becomes a man." Du Bois, with Douglass very much on his mind, transmuted chiasmus a half century later into the metaphor of duality or double consciousness, a necessary condition of living one's life, as he memorably put it, behind a "veil."

Du Bois's metaphor has a powerful legacy in twentieth century black fiction: James Weldon Johnson, in *Ex-Colored Man*, literalizes the trope of double consciousness by depicting as his protagonist a man who, at will, can occupy two distinct racial spaces, one black, one white, and who moves seamlessly, if ruefully between them. Toomer's *Cane* takes Du Bois's metaphor of duality for the inevitably split consciousness that every Negro must feel living in a country in which her or his status as a citizen is liminal at best, or has been erased at worst, and makes of this the metaphor for the human condition itself under modernity, a tellingly bold rhetorical gesture— one designed to make the Negro the metaphor of the human condition. And Hurston, in *Their Eyes*, extends Toomer's revision even further, depicting a character who can only gain her voice once she can name this condition of duality or double consciousness and then glide gracefully and lyrically between her two selves, an "inside" self and an "outside" one.

More recently, Alice Walker, in *The Color Purple*, signifies upon two aspects of the narrative strategy of *Their Eyes*: first, she revisits the theme of a young black woman finding her voice, depicting a protagonist who writes herself into being through letters addressed to God and to her sister, Nettie—letters that grow ever more sophisticated in their syntax and grammar and imagery as she comes to consciousness before our very eyes, letter to letter; and second, Walker riffs on Hurston's use of a vernacular-inflected free indirect discourse to show that black English has the capacity to serve as the medium for narrating a novel through the black dialect that forms a most pliable and expansive language in Celie's letters. Ralph Ellison makes Du Bois's metaphor of the veil a trope of blindness and life underground for his protagonist in *Invisible Man*, a protagonist who, as he types the story of his life from a hole underground, writes himself into being in the first person (in contradistinction to Richard Wright's protagonist, Bigger Thomas, whose reactive tale of fear and flight is told in the third person). Walker's novel also riffs on Ellison's claim for the revolutionary possibilities of writing the self into being, whereas Hurston's protagonist, Janie, speaks herself into being. Ellison himself signified multiply upon Richard Wright's *Native Son*, from the title to the use of the first-person bildungsroman to chart the coming to consciousness of a sensitive protagonist moving from blindness and an inability to do little more than react to his environment, to the insight gained by wresting control of his identity from social forces and strong individuals that would circumscribe and confine his life choices. Toni Morrison, master supernaturalist and perhaps the greatest black novelist of all, trumps Ellison's trope of blindness by returning over and over to the possibilities and limits of insight within worlds confined or circumscribed not by supraforces (à la Wright) but by the confines of the imagination and the ironies of individual and family history, signifying upon Faulkner, Woolf, and Márquez in the process. And Ishmael Reed, the father of black postmodernism and what we might think of as the hip-hop novel, the tradition's master parodist, signifies upon everybody and everything in the black literary tradition, from the slave narratives to the Harlem Renaissance to black nationalism and feminism.

This sort of literary signifying is what makes a literary tradition, well, a "tradition," rather than a simple list of books whose authors happen to have been born in the same country, share the same gender, or would be identified by their peers as belonging to this ethnic group or that. What makes these books special—"classic"—however, is something else. Each text has the uncanny capacity to take the seemingly mundane details of the day-to-day African American experience of its time and transmute those details and the characters' actions into something that transcends its ostensible subject's time and place, its specificity. These texts reveal the human universal through the African American particular: all true art, all classics, do this; this is what "art" is, a revelation of that which makes each of us sublimely human, rendered in the minute details of the actions and thoughts and feelings of a compelling character embedded in a time and place. But as soon as we find ourselves turning to a text for its anthropological or sociological data, we have left the realm of art; we have reduced the complexity of fiction or poetry to an essay, and this is not what imaginative literature is for. Richard Wright, at his best, did this, as did his signifying disciple Ralph Ellison; Louis Armstrong and Duke Ellington, Bessie Smith and Billie Holiday achieved this effect in music; Jacob Lawrence and Romare Bearden achieved it in the visual arts. And this is what Wole Soyinka does in his tragedies, what Toni Morrison does in her novels, what Derek Walcott does in his poetry. And while it is risky to name one's contemporaries in a list such as this, I think that Rita Dove and Jamaica Kincaid achieve this effect as well, as do Colson Whitehead and Edwidge Danticat, in a younger generation. (There are other writers whom I would include in this group had I the space.) By delving ever so deeply into the particularity of the African and African American experience, these authors manage, somehow, to come out the other side, making the race or the gender of their characters almost translucent, less important than the fact that they stand as aspects of ourselves beyond race or gender or time or place, precisely in the same magical way that Hamlet never remains for long stuck as a prince in a court in Denmark.

Each classic black text reveals to us, uncannily, subtly, how the Black Experience is inscribed, inextricably and indelibly, in the human experience, and how the human experience takes one of its myriad forms in blackface, as it were. Together, such texts also demonstrate, implicitly, that African American culture is one of the world's truly great and eternal cultures, as noble and as resplendent as any.

New Black Scribe

TERRY McMILLAN

In Afro-American Literature class, to discover that our lives
held as much significance and importance as our white
counterparts was more than gratifying, it was exhilarating.

Novelist Terry McMillan was born in 1951 in Port Huron, Michigan.
A journalism graduate of the University of California, Berkeley, who
became a tenured college professor at the University of Arizona at Tuc-
son, McMillan experienced phenomenal success with her third work of
fiction, *Waiting to Exhale*. Many in the book business credit her 1992
breakout bestseller and the following critically acclaimed *How Stella Got
Her Groove Back* with serving as the catalyst for changing the face of
publishing to a more expanded embrace of authors of color.

Now the author of about a dozen books, McMillan states at the end
of the following piece, "film school didn't work out." Fortunately to the
contrary, since she wrote this essay for the introduction to her 1990
anthology *Breaking Ice*, she has put her Columbia University master's
program education in filmmaking to good use as the screenwriter or the
script consultant for the movie adaptations of several of her bestselling
novels.

As a child, I didn't know that African American people wrote books. I grew up in a small town in northern Michigan, where the only books I came across were the Bible and required reading for school. I did not read for pleasure, and it wasn't until I was sixteen when I got a job shelving books at the public library that I got lost in a book. It was a biography of Louisa May Alcott. I was excited because I had not really read about poor white folks before; her father was so eccentric and idealistic that at the time I just thought he was crazy. I related to Louisa because she had to help support her family at a young age, which was what I was doing at the library.

Then one day I went to put a book away, and saw James Baldwin's face staring up at me. "Who in the world is this?" I wondered. I remember feeling embarrassed and did not read his book because I was too afraid. I couldn't imagine that he'd have anything better or different to say than Thomas Mann, Henry Thoreau, Ralph Waldo Emerson, Nathaniel Hawthorne, Ernest Hemingway, William Faulkner, etc. and a horde of other mostly white male writers that I'd been introduced to in Literature 101 in high school. I mean, not only had there not been any African American authors included in any of those textbooks, but I'd never been given a clue that if we did have anything important to say that somebody would actually publish it. Needless to say, I was not just naïve, but had not yet acquired an ounce of black pride. I never once questioned why there were no representative works by us in any of those textbooks. After all, I had never heard of any African American writers, and no one I knew hardly read *any* books.

And then things changed.

It wasn't until after Malcolm X had been assassinated that I found out who he was. I know I should be embarrassed about this, but I'm not. I read Alex Haley's biography of him and it literally changed my life. First and foremost, I realized that there was no reason to be ashamed of being black, that it was ridiculous. That we had a history, and much to be proud of. I began to notice how we had actually been treated as less than human; began to see our strength as a people whereas I'd only been made aware of our inferiorities. I started thinking about my role in the world and not just on my street. I started *thinking*. Thinking about things I'd never thought of before, and the thinking turned into questions. But I had more questions than answers.

So I went to college. When I looked through the catalog and saw a class called Afro-American Literature, I signed up and couldn't wait for the first day of class. Did *we* really have enough writers to warrant an entire class? I remember the textbook was called *Dark Symphony: Negro Literature in America* because I still have it. I couldn't believe the rush I felt over and over once I discovered Countee Cullen, Langston Hughes, Ann Petry, Zora Neale Hurston, Ralph Ellison, Jean Toomer, Richard Wright, and rediscovered and read James Baldwin, to name just a few. I'm surprised I didn't need glasses by the end of the semester. My world opened up. I accumulated and gained a totally new insight about, and perception of, our lives as "black" people, as if I had been an outsider and was finally let in. To discover that our lives held as much significance and importance as our white counterparts was more than gratifying, it was exhilarating. Not only had we lived diverse, interesting, provocative, and relentless lives, but during, through, and as a result of all these painful experiences, some folks had taken the time to write it down.

Not once, throughout my entire four years as an undergraduate did it occur to me that I might one day *be* a writer. I mean, these folks had genuine knowledge and insight. They also had a fascination with the truth. They had something to write about. Their work was bold, not flamboyant. They learned how to exploit the language so that readers would be affected by what they said and how they said it. And they had talent.

I never considered myself to be in possession of many of the above, and yet when I was twenty years old, the first man I fell in love with broke my heart. I was so devastated and felt so helpless that my reaction manifested itself in a poem. I did not sit down and say, "I'm going to write a poem about this." It was more like magic. I didn't even know I was writing a poem until I had written it. Afterward, I felt lighter, as if something had happened to lessen the pain. And when I read this "thing" I was shocked because I didn't know where the words came from. I was scared, to say the least, about what I had just experienced, because I didn't understand what had happened.

For the next few days, I read that poem over and over in disbelief because *I* had written it. One day, a colleague saw it lying on the kitchen table and read it. I was embarrassed and shocked when he said he liked it, then went on to tell me that he had just started a black literary magazine at the college and he wanted to publish it. Publish it? He was serious and it found its way onto a typeset page.

Seeing my name in print excited me. And from that point on, if a leaf moved on a tree, I wrote a poem about it. If a crack in the sidewalk glistened, surely there was a poem in that. Some of these verbose things actually got published in various campus newspapers that were obviously desperate to fill up space. I did not call myself a poet; I told people I wrote poems.

Years passed.

Those poems started turning into sentences and I started getting nervous. What the hell did I think I was doing? Writing these little go-nowhere vignettes. All these beginnings. And who did I think I was, trying to tell a story? And who cared? Even though I had no idea what I was doing, all I knew was that I was beginning to realize that a lot of things mattered to me, things disturbed me, things that I couldn't change. Writing became an outlet for my dissatisfactions, distaste, and my way of trying to make sense of what I saw happening around me. It was my way of trying to fix what I thought was broken. It later became the only way to explore personally what I didn't understand. The problem, however, was that I was writing more about ideas than people. Everything was so "large," and eventually I had to find a common denominator. I ended up asking myself what I really cared about: it was people, and particularly African American people.

The whole idea of taking myself seriously as a writer was ter-

rifying. I didn't know any writers. Didn't know how you knew if
you "had" it or not. Didn't know if I was or would ever be good
enough. I didn't know how you went about the business of writing, and besides, I sincerely wanted to make a decent living. (I had
read the horror stories of how so few writers were able to live off of
their writing alone, many having lived like bohemians.) At first, I
thought being a social worker was the right thing to do, since I was
bent on saving the world (I was an idealistic twenty-two years old),
but when I found I couldn't do it that way, I had to figure out another way to make an impact on folks. A positive impact. I ended
up majoring in journalism because writing was "easy" for me, but
it didn't take long for me to learn that I did not like answering the
"who, what, when, where, and why" of anything. I then—upon the
urging of my mother and friends who had graduated and gotten
"normal" jobs—decided to try something that would still allow me
to "express myself" but was relatively safer, though still risky: I went
to film school. Of course what was inherent in my quest to find my
"spot" in the world was this whole notion of affecting people on
some grand scale. Malcolm and Martin caused me to think like this.
Writing for me, as it's turned out, is philanthropy. It didn't take years
for me to realize the impact that other writers' work had had on me,
and if I was going to write, I did not want to write inconsequential,
mediocre stories that didn't conjure up or arouse much in a reader.
So I had to start by exciting myself and paying special attention to
what I cared about, what mattered to me.

Film school didn't work out. Besides, I never could stop writing,
which ultimately forced me to stop fighting it. It took even longer
to realize that writing was not something you aspired to be, it was
something you did because you had to.

THE PLEASURE

1968–2017

Authors born in the post–Baby Boom years share the current challenges and joys of self-expression and literary diversity.

MFA vs. POC

JUNOT DÍAZ

In my workshop, race was the unfortunate condition of nonwhite people that had nothing to do with white people and as such was not a natural part of the Universal of Literature.

Junot Díaz was born in the Dominican Republic in 1968 and raised in New Jersey. He is the author of the critically acclaimed *Drown*; *The Brief Wondrous Life of Oscar Wao*, which won the 2008 Pulitzer Prize and the National Book Critics Circle Award; and *This Is How You Lose Her*, a *New York Times* bestseller and National Book Award finalist. He is the recipient of a MacArthur "Genius" Fellowship, PEN/Malamud Award, Dayton Literary Peace Prize, Guggenheim Fellowship, and PEN/O. Henry Award. A graduate of Rutgers College, Díaz is the fiction editor at *Boston Review* and the Rudge and Nancy Allen Professor of Writing at the Massachusetts Institute of Technology.

He is also the cofounder of the writers' workshop Voices of Our Nation Arts Foundation (VONA), founded in 1999 in the San Francisco Bay Area, which endeavors to develop and support writers of color. In this adaptation of the introduction to *Dismantle: An Anthology of Writing from the VONA / Voices Writing Workshop*, Díaz shares his personal experience in a master of fine arts program that inspired the need for the founding of VONA and its mission to change the landscape for writers of color.

W hen I was in my mid-twenties I decided to apply for an MFA in creative writing. Part of it was I wanted to get *serious* with my writing—whatever that meant. Part of it was that my body was getting worn out from delivering pool tables. Part of it was a worrying sense I had that I was going to need a lot more sophistication if I was ever going to be any good at writing. And part of it was I didn't know I had other options.

These days there are all sorts of writing workshops: part-time, full-time, low-residency, and more resources online than you can shake a stick at. These days you got *fifth graders* that can talk your ears off about MFAs. This is the Age of the Writing Program—but in the early 90s none of that had come to pass. I barely knew what an MFA was. My professor told me some stuff, but these things are like the Matrix—no one can really *tell* you what they are; you have to experience them for yourself. Still, I was pretty dumb about the whole thing. I never visited the schools I applied to, didn't look up their faculty or try to communicate with any of their students. I went after it with about the same amount of foresight that my parents brought to their immigration—which from my perspective seemed to be none.

I applied blindly and not very widely.

Six programs, and out of some strange pocket of luck that the Universe reserves for total fools I got into one: Cornell. The plan was to spend two years in workshop, learning all I could about fiction in what I assumed was going to be a supportive environment.

I should have known better but hey I was young; I was naïve.

2

I didn't have a great workshop experience. Not at all. In fact by the start of my second year I was like: *get me the fuck out of here.*

So what was the problem?

Oh just the standard problem of MFA programs.
That shit was *too white.*

3

Some of you understand completely. And some of you ask: *Too white . . .* how?

Too white as in Cornell had almost no POC—no people of color—in it. Too white as in the MFA had no faculty of color in the fiction program—like none—and neither the faculty nor the administration saw that lack of color as a big problem. (At least the students are diverse, they told us.) Too white as in my workshop reproduced exactly the dominant culture's blind spots and assumptions around race and racism (and sexism and heteronormativity, etc). In my workshop there was an almost lunatical belief that race was no longer a major social force (it's class!). In my workshop we never explored our racial identities or how they impacted our writing—at all. Never got any kind of instruction in that area—at all. Shit, in my workshop we never talked about race except on the rare occasion someone wanted to argue that "race discussions" were exactly the discussion a serious writer should *not* be having.

From what I saw the plurality of students and faculty had been educated exclusively in the tradition of writers like William Gaddis, Francine Prose, or Alice Munro—and not at all in the traditions of Toni Morrison, Cherrie Moraga, Maxine Hong-Kingston, Arundhati Roy, Edwidge Danticat, Alice Walker, or Jamaica Kincaid. In my workshop the default subject position of reading and writing—of Literature with a capital L—was white, straight and male. This white straight male default was of course not biased in any way by its white straight maleness—no way! Race was the unfortunate condition of nonwhite people that had nothing to do with white people and as such was not a natural part of the Universal of Literature, and anyone that tried to introduce racial consciousness to the Great (White) Universal of Literature would be seen as politicizing the Pure Art and betraying the (White) Universal (no race) ideal of True Literature.

In my workshop what was defended was not the writing of people of color but the right of the white writer to write about people of color without considering the critiques of people of color.

Oh, yes: *too white* indeed. I could write pages on the unbearable too-whiteness of my workshop—I could write folio, octavo and duodecimo on its terrible whiteness—but you get the idea.

Simply put: I was a person of color in a workshop whose theory of reality did not include my most fundamental experiences as a person of color—that did not in other words include *me*.

No wonder I was unhappy in workshop. No wonder me and some of the other Calibans in the program—my Diné buddy, who I'll call Ichabod, and this Caribbean-American sister, who I'll call Athena—talked constantly about the workshop's race problem, about the shit our peers said to us (shit like: Why is there even Spanish in this story? Or: I don't want to write about race, I want to write about *real* literature). No wonder we all talked at one time or another of dropping out.

Some of you are probably saying: Fool, what did you expect?

That's a good question. I guess I assumed that a graduate program full of artists dedicated to seeing beyond the world's masks would be better on the race front—that despite all my previous experience with white-majority institutions the workshop would be an *exception*. What can I tell you? In those days I must have needed that little fantasy, that little hope that somewhere shit might be better.

Like I said: I was young.

4

It's been twenty years since my workshop days and yet from what I gather a lot of shit remains more or less the same. I've worked in two MFA programs and visited at least 30 others and the signs are all there. The lack of diversity of the faculty. Many of the students' lack of awareness of the lens of race, the vast silence on these matters in many workshops. I can't tell you how often students of color seek me out during my visits or approach me after readings in order to share with me the racist nonsense they're facing in their programs, from both their peers and their professors. In the last 17 years I must have had at least three hundred of these conversations, *minimum*. I remember one young MFA'r describing how a fellow writer (white) went through his story and erased all the "big" words because, said the peer, that's not the way "Spanish" people talk. This white peer, of course, had never lived in Latin America or Spain or in any US Latino community—he just knew. The workshop professor never corrected or even questioned said peer either. Just let the idiocy ride. Another young sister told me that in the entire two years of her workshop the only time people of color showed up in her white peers' stories was when crime or drugs were somehow involved. And when she tried to bring up the issue in class, tried to suggest readings that might illuminate the madness, her peers shut her down, saying *Our workshop is about writing, not political correctness.* As always race was the student of color's problem, not the white class's. Many of the writers I've talked to often finish up by telling me they're considering quitting their programs. Of course I tell them not to. If you can, please hang in there. We need your work. Desperately.

Sometimes they say: You did an MFA. Did you ever think about dropping out?

All the time.

Why didn't you?

5

Another good question. I'm not sure I have a real answer. Answers yes but An Answer: no. Maybe it was immigrant shit. Maybe it was characterological—I was just a stubborn fuck. Maybe it was the fact that I didn't want to move back to my mother's basement for anything. Maybe I just got lucky—I didn't snap or fall into a deep depression or get completely demoralized.

In all honesty I probably would have blown it eventually, the way I was drinking and acting out, but then at the start of my second year something happened. A massive Latino student movement sparked up on campus. That shit almost *never* happens but there it was, the real deal and, desperate for anything like a community, I jumped right the fuck in. That solidarity more or less saved my life. Made everything in workshop bearable because I suddenly had a group of people on campus who pulled for me, a group of people who *saw* me. Not a bad movement either—we scored some solids against the University and that also gives you a ton of heart. (One of our crowning triumphs, something I still take pride in, was that we were able to push through our first fiction faculty of color in the MFA program, Helena Maria Viramontes—how perfect is that? If I wrote it in a book no one would believe it—too pat—but that's exactly what happened. Helena came to campus too late for me but not for all the other students who have since benefited from her genius. Helena was exactly the faculty I had dreamed about during my MFA; she came out of the tradition of Chicana feminist artists, of women of color artists, the tradition of resistance, and in her workshop you better believe race existed and was not an interloper or an aberration from True Literature; it's a social force which all of us must learn to bear witness to.)

I think in the end it probably *was* the organizing. Got me refocused, gave me hope and energy. I did it; I graduated. My boy, Ichabod got through too—mostly by spending nearly every weekend away at the various upstate New York reservations. Athena, though, did not make it.

Talk about tragedy. Athena was a truly gifted writer. Wrote about her Island and its diaspora, their beauty and agonies with a clarity and sympathy I've never seen matched. She was also about the only ally I had in my actual workshop and one of the people in workshop who had the greatest impact on how I write today.

She was tough and she was smart and she'd read loads but in the end, the whiteness of the workshop just wore her out. These people are killing me, she told me repeatedly.

Word, I said. Word.

I thought that she was in the same place as all of us but one day she announced that she was quitting for real.

I'm done, she said.

Maybe she just decided to do other things. Maybe there were problems at home. Maybe she was tired.

I cannot honestly say.

Of course I tried to get her to stay. Shit, I would have gotten on my knees if I thought it would have changed her mind. Selfish shit really; I just didn't want to be alone in that workshop but she didn't change her mind. When push came to shove, none of us Calibans were close enough, I guess, to really make an intervention. Instead of pulling together we Calibans had all descended into our own spaces, taking the bus home every chance we got.

Early that fall (I think) Athena moved home; and I have never heard from her again. Shortly after a second writer of color left our workshop but I didn't know him at all (see how awesomely close we were) so I'm not going to speculate on the reasons. Still. The fact that we lost two writers of color in less than two years should tell you something.

Every now and then I search for signs of her writing on the Internet, but I don't think she's ever published anything. Breaks my heart because she was amazing.

6

Twenty years since the workshop and what I'm left with now is not bitterness or anger but an abiding sense of loss. Lost time, lost opportunities, lost people. When I think on it now what's most clear to me is how easily ours could have been a dope workshop. What might have been if we'd had one sympathetic faculty in our fiction program. If we Calibans hadn't all retreated into our separate bolt holes. If we'd actually been there for each other. What might have been if the other writers of color in the workshop—the ones who were like *I don't want to write about race*—had at least been open to discussing why that might be the case. I wonder what work might have been produced had we writers of colors been able to talk across our connections and divides, if we'd all felt safe and accounted for in the workshop, if we'd all been each other's witnesses. What might have been.

7

Lately I've been reading about MFA vs NYC. But for many of us it's MFA vs POC.

8

To fast-forward: in the end I became a published writer and one of the first things I did with that privilege was join some comrades to help found a workshop for writers of color. The Voices of Our Nation Workshop. A kind of Cave Canem, but for all genres and all people of color. Something right out of my wildest MFA dreams, where writers of color could gather to develop our art in a safe supportive environment. Where our ideas, critiques, concerns, our craft and, above all, *our experiences* would be privileged rather than marginalized; encouraged rather than ignored; discussed intelligently rather than trivialized. Where our contributions were not an adjunct to Literature but its core.

We're on our fourteenth year now and the workshop has become a lot of things. We're a thriving community of artists. We're a space of learning, of personal growth and yes, at times, of healing. For many of our participants we're a much-needed antidote to the oppressive biases of mainstream workshops.

But the workshop is deeper things too. Silent things we almost never talk about. For me it's an attempt to do over that lousy MFA I had. To create in the present a fix to a past that can never be altered.

It's also about Athena. I guess there's a simplistic foolish part of me that believes that if Athena had only had a workshop like ours she would never have quit. The workshop would have given her enough light to make it through. And we'd all be reading her today.

I guess I'm hoping one day she'll find us. And if there are other Athenas out there—which I know there are—I hope they find us too.

Create Dangerously

EDWIDGE DANTICAT

Some immigrant artists who might have had a
mother and father killed by a government or by
nature think we are accidents of literacy.

Edwidge Danticat was born in Haiti in 1969 and moved to the United
States when she was twelve. A graduate of Barnard College, she received
an MFA from Brown University.

Danticat is the author of many novels, including her debut, *Breath,
Eyes, Memory*, published to literary acclaim in 1996. Her first story
collection, *Krik? Krak!*, was nominated for a National Book Award, making her the youngest nominee ever. In 2013 a volume of interlocking
stories, *Claire of the Sea Light*, was published. *Brother, I'm Dying* was
a finalist for the National Book Award and winner of the National Book
Critics Circle Award for autobiography. Another nonfiction work, *The Art
of Death: Writing the Final Story*, published in 2017, is one of a series of
books from Graywolf Press on the craft of writing. In 2009, she received
a MacArthur Fellowship.

Create Dangerously: The Immigrant Artist at Work is a collection of
essays (from the Toni Morrison Lecture Series at Princeton University)
from which was excerpted this title story of how the assassinations of
two Haitian journalists had an impact on Danticat's perception of the
meaning and purpose of writing—to bear witness.

On November 12, 1964, in Port-au-Prince, Haiti, a huge crowd gathered to witness an execution. The president of Haiti at that time was the dictator François "Papa Doc" Duvalier, who was seven years into what would be a fifteen-year term. On the day of the execution he decreed that government offices be closed so that hundreds of state employees could be in the crowd. Schools were shut down and principals ordered to bring their students. Hundreds of people from outside the capital were bused in to watch.

The two men to be executed were Marcel Numa and Louis Drouin. Marcel Numa was a tall, dark-skinned twenty-one-year-old. He was from a family of coffee planters in a beautiful southern Haitian town called Jérémie, which is often dubbed the "city of poets." Numa had studied engineering at the Bronx Merchant Academy in New York and had worked for an American shipping company.

Louis Drouin, nicknamed Milou, was a thirty-one-year-old light-skinned man who was also from Jérémie. He had served in the U.S. army—at Fort Knox, and then at Fort Dix in New Jersey—and had studied finance before working for French, Swiss, and American banks in New York. Marcel Numa and Louis Drouin had been childhood friends in Jérémie.

The men had remained friends when they'd both moved to New York in the 1950s, after François Duvalier came to power. There they had joined a group called Jeune Haiti, or Young Haiti, and were two of thirteen Haitians who left the United States for Haiti in 1964 to engage in a guerrilla war that they hoped would eventually topple the Duvalier dictatorship.

The men of Jeune Haiti spent three months fighting in the hills and mountains of southern Haiti and eventually most of them died in battle. Marcel Numa was captured by members of Duvalier's army while he was shopping for food in an open market, dressed as a peasant. Louis Drouin was wounded in battle and asked his friends to leave him behind in the woods.

"According to our principles I should have committed suicide in that situation," Drouin reportedly declared in a final statement at his secret military trial. "Chandler and Guerdès [two other Jeune Haiti members] were wounded . . . the first one asked . . . his best friend to finish him off; the second committed suicide after destroying a case of ammunition and all the documents. That did not affect me. I reacted only after the disappearance of Marcel Numa, who had been sent to look for food and for some means of escape by sea. We were very close and our parents were friends."

After months of attempting to capture the men of Jeune Haiti and after imprisoning and murdering hundreds of their relatives, Papa Doc Duvalier wanted to make a spectacle of Numa and Drouin's deaths.

So on November 12, 1964, two pine poles are erected outside the national cemetery. A captive audience is gathered. Radio, print, and television journalists are summoned. Numa and Drouin are dressed in what on old black-and-white film seems to be the clothes in which they'd been captured—khakis for Drouin and a modest white shirt and denim-looking pants for Numa. They are both marched from the edge of the crowd toward the poles. Their hands are tied behind their backs by two of Duvalier's private henchmen, Tonton Macoutes in dark glasses and civilian dress. The Tonton Macoutes then tie the ropes around the men's biceps to bind them to the poles and keep them upright. . . .

A young white priest in a long robe walks out of the crowd with a prayer book in his hands. It seems that he is the person everyone has been waiting for. The priest says a few words to Drouin, who slides his body upward in a defiant pose. Drouin motions with his head toward his friend. The priest spends a little more time with Numa, who bobs his head as the priest speaks. If this is Numa's extreme unction, it is an abridged version.

The priest then returns to Drouin and is joined there by a stout Macoute in plain clothes and by two uniformed policemen, who lean in to listen to what the priest is saying to Drouin. It is possible that they are all offering Drouin some type of eye or face cover that he's refusing. Drouin shakes his head as if to say, let's get it over with. No blinders or hoods are placed on either man.

The firing squad, seven helmeted men in khaki military uniforms, stretch out their hands on either side of their bodies. They touch each other's shoulders to position and space themselves. The police and army move the crowd back, perhaps to keep them from being hit by ricocheted bullets. The members of the firing squad pick up their Springfield rifles, load their ammunition, and then place their weapons on their shoulders. Off screen someone probably shouts, "Fire!" and they do. Numa and Drouin's heads slump sideways at the same time, showing that the shots have hit home. . . .

All artists, writers among them, have several stories—one might call them creation myths—that haunt and obsess them. This is one of mine. I don't even remember when I first heard about it. I feel as though I have always known it, having filled in the curiosity-driven details through photographs, newspaper and magazine articles, books, and films as I have gotten older.

Like many a creation myth, aside from its heartrending clash of life and death, homeland and exile, the execution of Marcel Numa and Louis Drouin involves a disobeyed directive from a higher authority and a brutal punishment as a result. If we think back to the biggest creation myth of all, the world's very first people, Adam and Eve, disobeyed the superior being that fashioned them out of chaos, defying God's order not to eat what must have been the world's most desirable apple. Adam and Eve were then banished from Eden, resulting in everything from our having to punch a clock to spending many long, painful hours giving birth.

The order given to Adam and Eve was not to eat the apple. Their ultimate punishment was banishment, exile from paradise. We, the storytellers of the world, ought to be more grateful than most that banishment, rather than execution, was chosen for Adam and Eve, for had they been executed, there would never have been another story told, no stories to pass on.

In his play *Caligula*, Albert Camus, from whom I borrow part of the title of this essay, has Caligula, the third Roman emperor, declare that it doesn't matter whether one is exiled or executed, but it is much more important that Caligula has the power to choose. Even before they were executed, Marcel Numa and Louis Drouin had already been exiled. As young men, they had fled Haiti with their parents when Papa Doc Duvalier had come to power in 1957 and had immediately targeted for arrest all his detractors and resistors in the city of poets and elsewhere.

Marcel Numa and Louis Drouin had new lives for themselves, becoming productive young immigrants in the United States. In addition to his army and finance experience, Louis Drouin was said to have been a good writer and the communications director of Jeune Haiti. In the United States, he contributed to a Haitian political journal called *Lambi*. Marcel Numa was from a family of writers. One of his male relatives, Nono Numa, had adapted the seventeenth-century French playwright Pierre Corneille's *Le Cid*, placing it in a Haitian setting. Many of the young men Numa and Drouin joined with to form Jeune Haiti had had fathers killed by Papa Doc Duvalier, and had returned, Le Cid and Hamlet-like, to revenge them.

Like most creation myths, this one too exists beyond the scope of my own life, yet it still feels present, even urgent. Marcel Numa and Louis Drouin were patriots who died so that other Haitians could live. They were also immigrants, like me. Yet, they had abandoned comfortable lives in the United States and sacrificed themselves for the homeland. One of the first things the despot Duvalier tried to take away from them was the mythic element of their stories. In the propaganda preceding their execution, he labeled them not Haitian, but foreign rebels, good-for-nothing *blans*.

———

At the time of the execution of Marcel Numa and Louis Drouin, my recently married, twenty-nine-year-old parents lived in Haiti, in a neighborhood called Bel Air, about a thirty-minute walk from the cemetery. Bel Air had a government-sponsored community center, a *centre d'étude*, where young men and women—but mostly

young men—went to study in the evenings, especially if they had
no electricity at home. Some of these young people—not my parents, but young people who studied at the center—belonged to a
book club, a reading group sponsored by the Alliance Française,
the French Institute. The book group was called Le Club de Bonne
Humeur, or the Good Humor Club. At the time, Le Club de
Bonne Humeur was reading Camus' play *Caligula* with an eye to
possibly staging it.

In Camus' version of Caligula's life, when Caligula's sister, who is
also his lover, dies, Caligula unleashes his rage and slowly unravels.
In a preface to an English translation of the play, Camus wrote, "I
look in vain for philosophy in these four acts. . . . I have little regard
for an art that deliberately aims to shock because it is unable to
convince."

After the executions of Marcel Numa and Louis Drouin, as the
images of their deaths played over and over in cinemas and on state-
run television, the young men and women of the Club de Bonne
Humeur, along with the rest of Haiti, desperately needed art that
could convince. They needed art that could convince them that they
would not die the same way Numa and Drouin did. They needed
to be convinced that words could still be spoken, that stories could
still be told and passed on. So, as my father used to tell it, these
young people donned white sheets as togas and they tried to stage
Camus' play—quietly, quietly—in many of their houses, where they
whispered lines like:

> Execution relieves and liberates. It is a universal tonic, just in
> precept as in practice. A man dies because he is guilty. A man is
> guilty because he is one of Caligula's subjects. Ergo all men are
> guilty and shall die. It is only a matter of time and patience.

The legend of the underground staging of this and other plays,
clandestine readings of pieces of literature, was so strong that years
after Papa Doc Duvalier died, every time there was a political
murder in Bel Air, one of the young aspiring intellectuals in the

neighborhood where I spent the first twelve years of my life might inevitably say that someone should put on a play. And because the uncle who raised me while my parents were in New York for two-thirds of the first twelve years of my life, because that uncle was a minister in Bel Air and had a church and school with some available space, occasionally some of these plays were read and staged, quietly, quietly, in the backyard of his church. . . .

When it was a crime to pick up a bloodied body on the street, Haitian writers introduced Haitian readers to Sophocles' *Oedipus Rex* and *Antigone*, which had been rewritten in Creole and placed in Haitian settings by the playwright Franck Fouché and the poet Felix Morisseau Leroy. This is where these writers placed their bets, striking a dangerous balance between silence and art.

How do writers and readers find each other under such dangerous circumstances? Reading, like writing, under these conditions is disobedience to a directive in which the reader, our Eve, already knows the possible consequences of eating that apple but takes a bold bite anyway.

How does that reader find the courage to take this bite, open that book? After an arrest, an execution? Of course he or she may find it in the power of the hushed chorus of other readers, but she can also find it in the writer's courage in having stepped forward, in having written, or rewritten, in the first place.

Create dangerously, for people who read dangerously. This is what I've always thought it meant to be a writer. Writing, knowing in part that no matter how trivial your words may seem, someday, somewhere, someone may risk his or her life to read them. Coming from where I come from, with the history I have—having spent the first twelve years of my life under both dictatorships of Papa Doc and his son, Jean-Claude—this is what I've always seen as the unifying principle among all writers. This is what, among other things, might join Albert Camus and Sophocles to Toni Morrison, Alice Walker, Osip Mandelstam, and Ralph Waldo Emerson to Ralph Waldo Ellison. Somewhere, if not now, then maybe years in the future, a future that we may have yet to dream of, someone may risk his or her life to read us. Somewhere, if not now, then maybe years in the future, we may also save someone's life, because they have given us a passport, making us honorary citizens of their culture. . . .

This is a part of my story that I have always wanted to understand better: my family's brief encounters with the pleasures and dangers of reading. I am at a great deficit here because, aside from my much older cousin Maxo, there were not many fanatical readers in my family that I know of, much less people who would risk their lives over a book. Perhaps at a time when one could be shot so easily, assassinated so publicly, not reading or writing was a survival mechanism. Still, sprinkles of other readers' stories continue to intrigue and thrill me. Young men and women who worshipped Euripides and Voltaire, George Sand and Colette and Haiti's own physician novelist, Jacques Stephen Alexis, who in April 1961, three years before Numa and Drouin were executed, had been ambushed and murdered trying to return from exile, some say, to help topple the Duvalier dictatorship.

No one in my family that I know of had witnessed Numa and Drouin's execution in person. Still they could not help, when it came up, talking about it, even if in the broadest of terms.

"It was a very tragic time," my mother now says.

"It was something that touched a generation," my minister uncle used to say.

They were patriots who died so the rest of us could live, is a line I borrowed from my father. My father was the one who, while lying on his deathbed in early 2005, first told me about the banned books and the plays. Only when he mentioned togas and Caesars, and an author with a name that sounds like *camion*, did I manage to find my way, among many other possible choices to Camus' *Caligula*. I could be wrong about this too, making connections only I believe are there.

The only book my parents and uncle have read more than once is the Bible. I used to fear their reading my books, worried about disappointing them. My stories do not hold a candle to having lived under a dictatorship for most of your adult life, to having your neighbors disappear and not being able even to acknowledge it, to being forced to act as though these neighbors had never existed at all. Reading, and perhaps ultimately writing, is nothing like living in a place and time where two very young men are killed in a way that is treated like entertainment.

Mourir est beau, to die is beautiful, declares the Haitian national anthem. But writing could never attain that kind of beauty. Or could it? Writing is nothing like dying in, for, and possibly with, your country.

When I first started returning as a public person, as an "author," to Haiti, a place where people trace your failures and successes along family lines, I was often asked if there were any writers in my family. If there were, I do not know. . . .

In "Create Dangerously," Camus writes: "Art cannot be a monologue. We are on the high seas. The artist, like everyone else, must bend to his oar, without dying if possible." In many ways, Numa and Drouin shared the destiny of many Haitian artists, particularly that of the physician-novelist Jacques Stephen Alexis, who wrote such beautiful prose that the first time I read his description of freshly baked bread, I raised the book closer to my nose to sniff it. Perhaps there are no writers in my family because they were too busy trying to find bread. Perhaps there are no writers in my family because they were not allowed to or could barely afford to attend a decrepit village school as children. Perhaps there are no artists in my family because they were silenced by the brutal directives of one dictatorship, or one natural disaster, after another. Perhaps, just as Alice Walker writes of her own forebears in her essay "In Search of Our Mothers' Gardens," my blood ancestors—unlike my literary ancestors—were so weather-beaten, terror-stricken, and maimed that they were stifled. As a result, those who somehow managed to create became, in my view, martyrs and saints.

"Instead of being perceived as whole persons," wrote Walker, "their bodies became shrines: what was thought to be their minds became temples suitable for worship. These crazy 'Saints' stared out at the world, wildly, like lunatics—or quietly, like suicides; and the 'God' that was in their gaze was as mute as a great stone." . . .

The immigrant artist shares with all other artists the desire to interpret and possibly remake his or her own world. So though we may not be creating as dangerously as our forebears—though we are not risking torture, beatings, execution, though exile does not threaten us into perpetual silence—still, while we are at work bodies are littering the streets somewhere. People are buried under rubble somewhere. Mass graves are being dug somewhere. Survivors are living in makeshift tent cities and refugee camps somewhere, shielding their heads from the rain, closing their eyes, covering their ears, to shut out the sounds of military "aid" helicopters. And still, many are reading, and writing, quietly, quietly.

While I was "at work" at 4:53 p.m., on January 12, 2010, the ground was shaking and killing more than two hundred thousand people in a 7.0 magnitude earthquake in Haiti. And even before the first aftershock, people were calling me asking, "Edwidge, what are you going to do? When are you going back? Could you come on television or on the radio and tell us how you feel? Could you write us fifteen hundred words or less?"

Perhaps this is why the immigrant artist needs to feel that he or she is creating dangerously even though she is not scribbling on prison walls or counting the days until a fateful date with an executioner. Or a hurricane. Or an earthquake.

Self-doubt is probably one of the stages of acclimation in a new culture. It's a staple for most artists. As immigrant artists for whom so much has been sacrificed, so many dreams have been deferred, we already doubt so much. It might have been simpler, safer to have become the more helpful doctors, lawyers, engineers our parents wanted us to be. When our worlds are literally crumbling, we tell ourselves how right they may have been, our elders, about our passive careers as distant witnesses.

Who do we think we are?

We think we are people who risked not existing at all. People who might have had a mother and father killed, either by a government or by nature, even before we were born. Some of us think we are accidents of literacy.

I do.

We think we are people who might not have been able to go to school at all, who might never have learned to read and write. We think we are the children of people who have lived in the shadows for too long. We sometimes even think that we are like the ancient Egyptians, whose gods of death demanded documentation of worthiness and acceptance before allowing them entry into the next world. Might we also be a bit like the ancient Egyptians in the way of their artists and their art, the pyramid and coffin texts, tomb paintings, and hieroglyphic makers?

One of the many ways a sculptor of ancient Egypt was described was as "one who keeps things alive." Before pictures were drawn and amulets were carved for ancient Egyptians' tombs, wealthy men and women had their slaves buried with them to keep them company in the next life. The artists who came up with these other types of memorial art, the art that could replace the dead bodies, may also have wanted to save lives. In the face of both external and internal destruction, we are still trying to create as dangerously as they, as though each piece of art were a stand-in for a life, a soul, a future. As the ancient Egyptian sculptors may have suspected, and as Marcel Numa and Louis Drouin surely must have believed, we have no other choice. . . .

I return . . . to my great-grandparents' graves, often by myself. The year before [one visit], my first novel, *Breath, Eyes, Memory*, had been chosen for Oprah Winfrey's famous book club, generously exposing the book to thousands more readers than I had ever dreamed or imagined. The novel attempts to tell the story of three generations of Haitian women. Ifé Caco, the grandmother, loses her husband to a chain gang. Martine Caco, the older daughter, as a teenager is raped by a brutal Tonton Macoute whose face she never sees. Atie Caco, Martine's sister, harbors a secret unrequited love for another woman. Sophie Caco, the granddaughter, the narrator of the book, is the child who is born as a result of her mother's rape. All of these women share a trauma: all had mothers who regularly inserted the tips of their fingers into their daughters' vaginas to check that they were still virgins.

The virginity testing element of the book led to a backlash in some Haitian American circles. "You are a liar," a woman wrote to me right before I left on the trip. "You dishonor us, making us sexual and psychological misfits."

"Why was she taught to read and write?" I overheard a man saying at the Haitian American fund-raising gala in New York, where I was getting an award for writing this book. "This is not us. The things she writes, they are not us."

Maligned as we were in the media at the time, as disaster-prone refugees and boat people and AIDS carriers, many of us had become overly sensitive and were eager to censor anyone who did not project a "positive image" of Haiti and Haitians.

The letter writer was right, though. I was lying in that first book and all the other pieces of fiction I have written since. But isn't that what the word *fiction* or *novel* on the book jacket had implied? Isn't even the most elementary piece of fiction about a singularly exceptional fictional person, so that even if that fictional person is presented as an everyman or everywoman, he or she is bound to be the most exceptional everyman or everywoman fictional person of the lot? And how can one individual—be it me or anyone else—know how nine to ten million other individuals should or would behave? Furthermore, though I was not saying that "testing" happened in every Haitian household, to every Haitian girl, I knew many women and girls who had been "tested" in that way.

"You are a parasite and you exploit your culture for money and what passes for fame," is the second most common type of criticism I get from inside the community.

Anguished by my own sense of guilt, I often reply feebly that in writing what I do, I exploit no one more than myself. Besides, what is the alternative for me or anyone else who might not dare to offend? Self-censorship? Silence?

During one of my visits to my great-grandparents' grave, I had with me a book of essays titled *Afterwords: Novelists on Their Novels,* which features several writers discussing their published novels. So, while I was sitting at the gravesite, I wrote the following letter to my first novel's main character, Sophie. And since the immigrant artist must sometimes apologize for airing, or appearing to air, dirty laundry, my note to Sophie was later published as an afterword in all subsequent editions of the book, becoming an addendum to the text.

Dear Sophie,

I am writing you this note while sitting on the edge of my great-grandmother's grave, an elevated tombstone in the high mountains of Léogâne, overlooking a majestic lime-colored mountain range. Suspended as I am here, far from terra firma and close to the clouds, I feel that this is the only place in the world where I truly belong. This is the place that I most wished as a home for you too, the place I had in mind when I had Tante Atie stand with you in the middle of a cemetery plot and pronounce, "Walk straight, you are in the presence of family."

I guess I have always felt, writing about you, that I was in the presence of family, a family full of kindness as well as harshness, a family full of love as well as grief, a family deeply rooted in the past yet struggling to confront an unpredictable future. I felt blessed to have encountered this family of yours, the Cacos, named after a bird whose wings look like flames. I feel blessed to have shared your secrets, your mother's, your aunt's, your grandmother's secrets, mysteries deeply embedded in you, in them, much like the wiry vetiver clinging to the side of these hills.

I write this to you now, Sophie, because your secrets, like you, like me, have traveled far from this place. Your experiences in the night, your grandmother's obsessions, your mother's "tests," have taken on a larger meaning and your body is now being asked to represent a larger space than your flesh. You are being asked, I have been told, to represent every girl child, every woman from this land that you and I love so much. Tired of protesting, I feel I must explain. Of course, not all Haitian mothers are like your mother. Not all Haitian daughters are tested as you have been.

　I have always taken for granted that this story, which is yours, and only yours, would always be read as such. But some of the voices that come back to me, to you, to these hills respond with a different kind of understanding than I had hoped. And so I write this to you now, Sophie, as I write it to myself, praying that the singularity of your experience be allowed to exist, along with your own peculiarities, inconsistencies, your own voice. And I write this note to you, thanking you for the journey of healing from here and back—that you and I have been through together with every step wishing that both our living and our dead will rest in peace.

May these words bring wings to your feet,
Edwidge Danticat
Summer 1999

How to Write

COLSON WHITEHEAD

Rule No. 10: Revise, revise, revise. I cannot stress this enough. Revision is when you do what you should have done the first time, but didn't.

Colson Whitehead was born in 1969; he was raised in Manhattan. After graduating from Harvard College, he worked at the *Village Voice*, where he wrote reviews of television, books, and music. His first novel, *The Intuitionist* (1999), concerned intrigue in the Department of Elevator Inspectors; it was a finalist for the PEN/Hemingway Award for Debut Fiction and a winner of the Quality Paperback Book Club's New Voices Award. Several award-winning novels have followed: *John Henry Days* in 2001, *Apex Hides the Hurt* (2006), *Sag Harbor* (2009), and *Zone One* (2011). *The Colossus of New York*, published in 2003, is a book of essays about the city. *The Noble Hustle: Poker, Beef Jerky & Death*, a nonfiction account of the 2011 World Series of Poker, appeared in 2014. *The Underground Railroad*, a novel, was published in 2016. It won the Pulitzer Prize, the National Book Award, the Carnegie Medal for Fiction, and was a #1 *New York Times* bestseller.

Whitehead's reviews, essays, and fiction have appeared in a number of publications, such as the *New York Times*, the *New Yorker*, *New York* magazine, *Harper's*, and *Granta*. He has received a MacArthur Fellowship, a Guggenheim Fellowship, a Whiting Writers Award, the Dos Passos Prize, and a fellowship at the Cullman Center for Scholars and Writers. He has taught at numerous colleges and universities, and lives in New York City.

In 2012, the *New York Times Book Review* published Whitehead's rules for writing.

Threshold art of writing can be reduced to a few simple rules. I share
them with you now.

Rule No. 1: Show and Tell. Most people say, "Show, don't
tell," but I stand by Show and Tell, because when writers put their
work out into the world, they're like kids bringing their broken
unicorns and chewed-up teddy bears into class in the sad hope that
someone else will love them as much as they do. "And what do you
have for us today, Marcy?" "A penetrating psychological study of
a young med student who receives disturbing news from a former
lover." "How marvelous! Timmy, what are you holding there?" "It's
a Calvinoesque romp through an unnamed metropolis much like
New York, narrated by an armadillo." "Such imagination!" Show
and Tell, followed by a good nap.

Rule No. 2: Don't go searching for a subject, let your subject find
you. You can't rush inspiration. How do you think Capote came to
"In Cold Blood"? It was just an ordinary day when he picked up the
paper to read his horoscope, and there it was—fate. Whether it's a
harrowing account of a multiple homicide, a botched Everest expe-
dition or a colorful family of singers trying to escape from Austria
when the Nazis invade, you can't force it. Once your subject finds
you, it's like falling in love. It will be your constant companion.
Shadowing you, peeping in your windows, calling you at all hours
to leave messages like, "Only you understand me." Your ideal subject
should be like a stalker with limitless resources, living off the inheritance he received after the suspiciously sudden death of his father.
He's in your apartment pawing your stuff when you're not around,
using your toothbrush and cutting out all the really good synonyms
from the thesaurus. Don't be afraid: you have a best seller on your
hands.

Rule No. 3: Write what you know. Bellow once said, "Fiction
is the higher autobiography." In other words, fiction is payback for
those who have wronged you. When people read my books "My
Gym Teacher Was an Abusive Bully" and "She Called Them Brussels

Sprouts: A Survivor's Tale," they're often surprised when I tell them they contain an autobiographical element. Therein lies the art, I say. How do you make that which is your everyday into the stuff of literature? Listen to your heart. Ask your heart, Is it true? And if it is, let it be. Once the lawyers sign off, you're good to go.

Rule No. 4: Never use three words when one will do. Be concise. Don't fall in love with the gentle trilling of your mellifluous sentences. Learn how to "kill your darlings," as they say. I'm reminded of the famous editor-author interaction between Gordon Lish and Ray Carver when they were working on Carver's celebrated short story "Those Life Preservers Are Just for Show," often considered the high-water mark of so-called dirty realism. You'll recall the climax, when two drunken fishermen try to calm each other after their dinghy springs a leak. In the original last lines of the story, Nat, the salty old part-time insurance agent, reassures his young charge as they cling to the beer cooler: "We'll get help when we hit land. I'm sure of it. No more big waves, no more sharks. We'll be safe once again. We'll be home." If you examine the Lish papers in the Lilly Library at Indiana University, you'll see how, with but a few deft strokes, Lish pared that down to create the now legendary ending: "Help—land shark!" It wasn't what Carver intended, but few could argue that it was not shorter. Learn to kill your darlings, and don't be shy about softening them up in the hostage pit for a few days before you do.

Rule No. 5: Keep a dream diary.

Rule No. 6: What isn't said is as important as what is said. In many classic short stories, the real action occurs in the silences. Try to keep all the good stuff off the page. Some "real world" practice might help. The next time your partner comes home, ignore his or her existence for 30 minutes, and then blurt out "That's it!" and drive the car onto the neighbor's lawn. When your children approach at bedtime, squeeze their shoulders meaningfully and, if you're a woman, smear your lipstick across your face with the back of your wrist, or, if you're a man, weep violently until they say, "It's O.K., Dad." Drink out of a chipped mug, a souvenir from a family vacation or weekend getaway in better times, one that can trigger a two-paragraph compare/contrast description later on. It's a bit like Method acting. Simply let this thought guide your every word and gesture: "Something is wrong—can you guess what it is?" If you're going for something a little more postmodern, repeat the above, but with fish.

Rule No. 7: Writer's block is a tool—use it. When asked why you haven't produced anything lately, just say, "I'm blocked." Since most people think that writing is some mystical process where characters "talk to you" and you can hear their voices in your head, being blocked is the perfect cover for when you just don't feel like working. The gods of creativity bless you, they forsake you, it's out of your hands and whatnot. Writer's block is like "We couldn't get a baby sitter" or "I ate some bad shrimp," an excuse that always gets you a pass. The electric company nagging you for money, your cell provider harassing you, whatever—just say, "I'm blocked," and you're off the hook. But don't overdo it. In the same way the baby-sitter bit loses credibility when your kids are in grad school, there's an expiration date. After 20 years, you might want to mix it up. Throw in an Ellisonian "My house caught fire and burned up my opus." The specifics don't matter—the important thing is to figure out what works for you.

Rule No. 8: Is secret.

Rule No. 9: Have adventures. The Hemingway mode was in ascendancy for decades before it was eclipsed by trendy fabulist "exercises." The pendulum is swinging back, though, and it's going to knock these effete eggheads right out of their Aeron chairs. Keep ahead of the curve. Get out and see the world. It's not going to kill you to butch it up a tad. Book passage on a tramp steamer. Rustle up some dysentery; it's worth it for the fever dreams alone. Lose a kidney in a knife fight. You'll be glad you did.

Rule No. 10: Revise, revise, revise. I cannot stress this enough. Revision is when you do what you should have done the first time, but didn't. It's like washing the dishes two days later instead of right after you finish eating. Get that draft counter going. Remove a comma and then print out another copy—that's another draft right there. Do this enough times and you can really get those numbers up, which will come in handy if someone challenges you to a draft-off. When the ref blows the whistle and your opponent goes, "26 drafts!," you'll bust out with "216!" and send 'em to the mat.

Rule No. 11: There are no rules. If everyone jumped off a bridge, would you do it, too? No. There are no rules except the ones you learned during your Show and Tell days. Have fun. If they don't want to be friends with you, they're not worth being friends with. Most of all, just be yourself.

From Jamaica to Minnesota to Myself

MARLON JAMES

*In creative writing, I teach that characters
arise out of our need for them.*

Marlon James was born in Jamaica in 1970. His novel *A Brief History of Seven Killings* (2014) was a finalist for the National Book Critics Circle Award and won the OCM Bocas Prize for Caribbean Literature for fiction, the Anisfield-Wolf Book Award for fiction, and the Minnesota Book Award. In addition, it was a *New York Times Notable Book*. James is also the author of *The Book of Night Women*, which won the 2010 Dayton Literary Peace Prize and the Minnesota Book Award and was a finalist for the 2010 National Book Critics Circle Award in fiction and an NAACP Image Award. His first novel, *John Crow's Devil*, was a finalist for the Los Angeles Times Book Prize for first fiction and the Commonwealth Writers' Prize and was a *New York Times Editors' Choice*. James lives in Minneapolis, where he is an associate professor of English at Macalester College.

In 2015, the *New York Times Magazine* published this essay by James on his literary journey.

had just left my parents' house in Portmore, a suburb outside Kingston, for my own apartment in the city: a one-bedroom studio, barely 600 square feet, with yellow shag carpeting, a tiny terrace enclosed in jail bars, a bedroom looking out on somebody else's bedroom and a ceiling I could reach. I locked myself away from the neighbors with two deadbolts.

At 28 years old, seven years out of college, I was so convinced that my voice outed me as a fag that I had stopped speaking to people I didn't know. The silence left a mark, threw my whole body into a slouch, with a concave chest, as if trying to absorb impact. I'd spent seven years in an all-boys school: 2,000 adolescents in the same khaki uniforms striking hunting poses, stalking lunchrooms, classrooms, changing rooms, looking for boys who didn't fit in. I bought myself protection by cursing, locking my lisp behind gritted teeth, folding away my limp wrist and drawing 36-double-D girls for art class. I took a copy of *Penthouse* to school to score cool points, but the other boys called me "batty boy" anyway—every day, five days a week. To save my older, cooler brother, I pretended we weren't related. At home, I lost myself in Dickens's London, Huck Finn's Mississippi River or Professor Xavier's School for Gifted Youngsters. One day after school, instead of going home, I walked for miles, all the way down to Kingston Harbor. I stopped right at the edge of the dock, thinking next time I would just keep walking.

The University of the West Indies was a door: wide open. I found friends who seemed to have been waiting all summer for me to show up. I walked into the library with a back issue of *Spin*, and somebody asked if that was the one with Tom Waits. I'd known people who were geeky, sarcastic, well versed in the Smiths and "The Wrath of Khan," but they had never been my friends before. Now I was dragged into word wars because one friend said "Time Bandits" was the greatest movie ever, when everybody knew it was "Life of Brian." There were cheap liquor, potato chips, ironic quips, mix tapes. But when college ended, I returned home, got a job in advertising and shut myself down again. The people I had left behind were waiting for me when I got back.

The entrance to my cubicle was blocked by a boss with curious eyebrows who asked why all my magazines showed men on the covers, what GQ meant, where was *Playboy*? Every man in the office had a woman on the side, whether he was married or not, and even monogamous men were considered gay. Memories of childhood returned as nightmares: I was a kid again, frightened by school, praying to God every night, *please let me wake up in another body*. One that walked and talked right. That did not play house with a boy in the neighborhood that time when he was 8 and I was 9 and ruin him and myself.

One day I bought "Steppenwolf," by Hermann Hesse, in a bookstore. Early in the book, an irrefutable argument for suicide jumped out and grabbed me by the neck: the scene in which the protagonist, having given himself his own expiration date, realizes that he can put up with anything, tolerate everything, suffer through all things because he knows when he's going to check out. I hadn't thought about killing myself since I was 16. But now there were nights when I woke up crying, or found myself out on the jail-terrace sunk so low into sadness that I had no memory of how I got there. I listened over and over again to lyrics from the song "I Found a Reason," by the Velvet Underground: "I do believe/If you don't like things you leave." I cried for a sorrow that I did not know I had.

I was 28 years old, and I'd reached the end of myself. Electric words, "end of yourself"—I first heard them during a sermon in a Kingston church. The preacher was talking about when you reached the limits of your own wisdom and the only person left with any answers was God. A new friend in the office, who went to school in Canada and came in as my assistant, read my sarcasm as a defense tactic, though he didn't know the reason, and said, "You should come to church this Sunday." By then I was having panic attacks. I went to a doctor and asked, "Am I normal?" He said normal was a scale, with the left being normal and the right being abnormal, and

I was somewhere on the left side of the middle. Then he gave me Xanax and asked if I wanted Prozac. Instead I got saved.

The church was called a clap-hands congregation, meaning charismatic, except it was full of upper-middle-class folk, and a cool pastor who drove a sports car. One Wednesday night, while Pastor was telling us that blessings were five miles upstream so we should, like Enoch, wait on the Lord, I started reading Salman Rushdie's "Shame," hiding it in the leather Bible case. I had never read anything like it. It was like a hand grenade inside a tulip. Its prose was so audacious, its reality so unhinged, that you didn't see at first how pointedly political and just plain furious it was. It made me realize that the present was something I could write my way out of. And so I started writing for the first time since college, but kept it quiet because none of it was holy. I stayed in church for nearly nine years, telling a woman I tried to date that the real reason I had no interest in a relationship was Jesus. In 2005, when I was 34, I published my first novel, "John Crow's Devil," and wrote myself all the way to a book tour of the United States.

I stepped off the 6 train at Spring Street. Black combat boots busting a move. The phrase is nearly 20 years old, true, but I claimed it because I needed it, never more than right then. Levi's Offender jeans sausaging my legs skinny; hip hug, butt squeeze, flaring below the knee and over my boots. Blue Stereolab T-shirt that stopped above the belt, Calvin Klein shades bought cheap at Century 21. Stepping out of the subway, emerging crotch first, posture moving from a slump like a question mark to a buffalo stance, an exclamation point. Walking to where Spring hits Broadway, the sexiest junction in all America, I'd heard. Where modeling agencies look down on modeling hopefuls strutting like peacocks.

Anonymity was a sea to dive into. Stonewall was a club to pass by—I was years away from having the guts to go in. Besides, I had no friends. In store windows, I saw a person who took me by surprise at first. The Strand Book Store, Tower Records, Other Music, Shakespeare & Co.; each was a step further away from the self I had left behind in another country.

It was getting dark, though summer stretches daylight, and I needed to be back in the Bronx. My younger half brother and his mother lived there, on a street of Jamaican immigrants. I walked to Barnes & Noble in Union Square, to the bathroom. I closed the door of the special-needs toilet, the same stall I used seven hours before, pulled my normal clothes out of the backpack and peeled New York off my skin. Back to loose T-shirt. Baggy jeans. Sneakers on my feet, boots in the bag. I took the 5 train home to the Bronx.

In creative writing, I teach that characters arise out of our need for them. By now, the person I created in New York was the only one I wanted to be. Over the next two years, I came and left often, pushing the limits of a student visa. I'd make friends but never get close enough to have them ask me anything too deep, playing at being aloof when I was really just shy, and I'd walk past gay bars, turn and walk past again, but never go in. Back home I fell back into church, knowing I didn't belong there anymore. Once I forgot to code-switch in time and dashed to the bathroom in J.F.K., minutes before my flight to Kingston, to change out of my skinny jeans and hoop earrings. Eight years after reaching the end of myself, I was on borrowed time. Whether it was in a plane or a coffin, I knew I had to get out of Jamaica.

Then the college called. Macalester, in St. Paul, Minnesota. They liked my application letter, résumé and first novel and wanted to interview me. Minnesota, though. My entire knowledge of that state came from Prince's movie "Purple Rain." Everyone I asked said only: "It's cold." In January, I flew to the U.S. for an interview, then back to Jamaica, and waited, trying to feel nothing, just to keep from being disappointed. In March, Macalester sent an email. A one-year teaching job, full time. I packed up my entire life—my books—to ship to the States. It may have been only a one-year contract, but I was never going back. I felt no emotion. I didn't see anything of Minnesota until the day I showed up for work.

I was shocked by my empty apartment, thinking "empty" meant a few chairs and a couch. I bought an air bed from Target. Seven days in, I put on jogging shoes and didn't stop running until I saw something I liked, the downtown Minneapolis skyline. For a man always fearing what people thought, I was suspicious of "Minnesota nice," everybody smiling and saying hello while they kept walking. But by the end of the first week, somebody I'd just met gave me a bicycle to get around; someone else bought me coffee mugs. Another professor, Casey, who moved here to teach as well, was into the band My Bloody Valentine *and* "Project Runway." We became friends in 36 hours. In less than a year, I moved out of school housing to my first real apartment, and a young man who was my neighbor knocked on my door, asking, "Hey, you wanna smoke a bowl with us?" His name was Alex, and his friend across the landing was John-John. Two handsome straight boys who adopted me and became partners in finding me a life, mostly by getting me drunk at the Irish bar up the road.

I had never set foot in a gay bar without paranoia pushing me back out. During Gay Pride week, Alex and John-John dragged me to one called Camp, which was decorated with disco balls and drawings of octopus tentacles. Alex dressed as a cowboy, John-John as Travolta in "Saturday Night Fever," both addressing themselves to people who hadn't asked as my "bitches." I was almost a cowboy, with a western shirt, vest and boot-cut jeans. I wasn't quite sure what was supposed to happen, and neither were they, so we just drank.

Three years later, my best friend, Ingrid, visited from Jamaica. She looked at my walls, covered with photos and posters, books all the way to the ceiling, four shelves of vinyl, copies of *GQ*, *Bookforum* and *Out* magazines scattered everywhere, my "simile is like a metaphor" T-shirt, then at my face and said: "This is so *you*, dude. I've never seen you as *you* before." I didn't even realize when it happened, when I stopped playing roles. I wore my New York clothes to class, on the street, to clubs. Nobody cared that my jeans had a nine-inch rise. I no longer looked over my shoulder in the dark.

I Once Was Miss America

ROXANE GAY

I am nearly forty, but my love of Sweet Valley remains
strong and immediate. When I read the books now,
I know I'm reading garbage, but I remember what it
was like to spend my afternoons in Sweet Valley.

Roxane Gay's writing has appeared in *Best American Mystery Stories
2014*, *Best American Short Stories 2012*, *Best Sex Writing 2012*, *A
Public Space*, *McSweeney's*, *Tin House*, *Oxford American*, *American
Short Fiction*, *West Branch*, *Virginia Quarterly Review*, *NOON*, the *New
York Times Book Review*, *Bookforum*, *Time*, the *Los Angeles Times*, the
Nation, the *Rumpus*, *Salon*, and many others. Born in 1974, the coedi-
tor of *PANK* is also the author of the books *Ayiti*, *An Untamed State*, *Bad
Feminist*, and *Hunger*.

In this excerpt from her 2014 *New York Times* bestselling collection
of essays, *Bad Feminist*, Gay lets us in on the enjoyment she experienced as a teenager reading her favorite young-adult novel series, Sweet
Valley High, and dreaming about following in the Miss America footsteps
of Vanessa Williams.

n 1984, Vanessa Williams became Miss America. She would later have to step down because of a nude photo scandal, but when she was first crowned it was an amazing moment for black girls everywhere. Williams was the first black woman to wear the Miss America crown in the pageant's sixty-three-year history. I was not the kind of girl who cared much about pageants or being a beauty queen, but watching Williams and her perfect cheekbones and glittering teeth as she accepted the crown gave girls like me ideas. That moment made us believe we too could be beautiful.

While Vanessa Williams offered black girls a new image of who the All-American Girl could be, the more traditional image of the All-American Girl could be found in Sweet Valley, an idyllic town in sunny Southern California where the lawns are perfectly manicured. Everyone is fit and beautiful and successful. As is the case in most perfect places, life in Sweet Valley is episodic. There is a narrative arc to each day or week or month, always a valuable lesson to be learned from life's experiences. The endings, in Sweet Valley, are mostly happy. The meek inherit. All good things come to those who wait. There is nowhere in the world like Sweet Valley.

Elizabeth and Jessica Wakefield are the sweethearts of Sweet Valley. They are blond and thin and perfect even with all their human flaws. The Wakefield sisters are twins—twice the perfection. Elizabeth is the good twin, and Jessica is the more rebellious twin. Jessica is a bad, bad girl, even though in Sweet Valley, a bad girl is never quite that bad. The sisters wear matching lavaliere necklaces, and they drive a red Fiat. Elizabeth and Jessica love each other and are best friends, but they are also rivals. Sisters are complicated even when they are perfect.

Elizabeth is responsible and universally adored for her sweetness and patience. She wants to be a journalist. She loves Todd Wilkins, a tall, handsome, and popular basketball player. She works on the school paper and is a cheerleader—smart and athletic, the perfect combination.

Jessica likes boys and partying. She is charming and enjoys gossip, flirting, and shopping. She loves to borrow Elizabeth's clothes, and Elizabeth puts up with it because you cannot say no to Jessica Wakefield. She's a cheerleader too, and although she comes off as a bit of an airhead, Jessica has depth and intelligence. She sometimes says unkind things, but that's because she is impulsive and has a bit of a temper. She's all emotion. Jessica is the kind of girl who gives in to her impulses, while Elizabeth controls her urges, at least most of the time.

The Wakefield twins aren't real; they are the main characters of the Sweet Valley High series. I started reading the Sweet Valley High books when I was eight or nine years old. I was cross-eyed and wore thick bifocals. Other than my younger brother, I was the only black kid in school, so I was going to be noticed even though I wanted very much to go unnoticed. I was shy and awkward and didn't know how to fix myself. My hair was wild, stood on end, earning me the inexplicable nicknames Hair, Beard, and Mustache even though I had neither a beard nor a mustache. My classmates also called me Don King. I looked nothing like Don King. He's a man, for one. I was told my parents "talked funny," which I later realized was a reference to their thick Haitian accents, which I did not hear until they were pointed out to me and then suddenly those accents were all I heard. I read books while I walked to school. I had the strangest laugh—somewhat halted and tentative—and a bit of a bucktooth situation. I regularly wore overalls by choice and didn't *really* know any curse words, so that should give you a sense of where I was on the social ladder—reaching for the bottom rung.

When I first started reading Sweet Valley High books, I wanted girls like the Wakefield twins to love me. I wanted the handsome boys who chased girls like those Wakefield twins to love me. I wanted the popular kids to pull me into the shelter of their golden embrace and make me popular too. Popularity is contagious. Many movies from the 1980s bear this theory out. I had hope, is what I'm saying, though certainly that hope was fragile.

There was one particular group of golden, popular kids at my school. They're in every school, an interchangeable infestation of good genes and big smiles and perfect hair and Guess or Girbaud jeans. I don't remember much about grade school, but I remember the first and last names of the popular kids. If I returned to my childhood neighborhood, I could point out their houses and other geographical points of interest. I watched the popular kids all the time, trying to figure out how to breathe the air in their atmosphere. They were so *American* and, therefore, exotic because they had freedoms I did not. I was a different kind of American. I had conservative Haitian parents who wanted the best for their kids but were also very wary of American permissiveness. I was American at school and Haitian at home. This required negotiating a fine balance, and I am a clumsy person.

There is nothing more desperate and unrequited than the love an unpopular girl nurtures for the cool kids. One day, the kids in the popular clique were teasing me, about what, I do not remember. I got angrier and angrier as they taunted me, not only because they were teasing me but also because I was so painfully aware of the gaping distance between where we were and where I wanted us to be—walking through the mall, arm in arm, or sharing secrets at a slumber party, or gossiping about cute boys. I liked the mall. I had secrets. I liked cute boys.

That day, though, I needed to come up with a snappy retort to show them they couldn't push me around, to show them I was cool too, to stand my ground. I pointed my fingers at them like Miss Celie laying a curse on Mister in *The Color Purple*, and I shouted, "One day, just you wait and see. I'm going to become Miss America." That was my mother's nickname for me, Miss America. I'm her beloved firstborn, her first child born in these United States. I loved my nickname. Those popular kids laughed and laughed. For the rest of that year and into the next, they teased me mercilessly about being Miss America, asking how my campaign was going, making comments about sashes and crowns, prancing around in front of me doing the Miss America wave. They incorporated props. Those kids made it clear I didn't have a shot in hell at the crown, but I'm stubborn and Vanessa Williams had won Miss America so I began to sincerely believe I was going to become Miss America. I reminded my classmates of my belief regularly, which only fueled their petty torments. I have no idea where I was going with that strategy. . . .

Like many writers, I lived inside of books as a child. Inside books I could get away from the impossible things I had to deal with. When I read I was never lonely or tormented or scared. I read everything I could get my hands on, and my parents indulged and encouraged me. They were strict about things like television and grades, but they never censored my reading material or questioned my love of Sweet Valley. We moved around a lot for my father's job, but Sweet Valley never moved and the people never changed. The kids in Sweet Valley were a constant, and in a small, poignant way, they were my friends.

I waited for new Sweet Valley High books the way other kids waited for new comics or movie releases. Each time my mother took me to the mall, I went straight to Waldenbooks and quickly scanned the shelves in the Young Adult section, wondering what the twins and their friends and enemies would get into next. When the series began churning out thick super editions, I could have died and gone to Sweet Valley heaven. As my collection of Sweet Valley High books grew, I maintained the set meticulously, keeping the books in perfect order and pristine condition. Sometimes my brothers would sneak into my room and reorder the books. Minor skirmishes would erupt between us that often ended with me doing something like burying their favorite toys in the backyard. I was quite serious about my Sweet Valley High books.

Nostalgia is powerful. It is natural, human, to long for the past, particularly when we can remember our histories as better than they were. Life happens faster than I can comprehend. I am nearly forty, but my love of Sweet Valley remains strong and immediate. When I read the books now, I know I'm reading garbage, but I remember what it was like to spend my afternoons in Sweet Valley, hanging out with the Wakefield twins and Enid Rollins and Lila Fowler and Bruce Patman and Todd Wilkins and Winston Egbert. The nostalgia I feel for these books and these people makes my chest ache.

When I learned that Francine Pascal was releasing *Sweet Valley Confidential*, an update to the Sweet Valley High series, set ten years into the future, I basically lost my shit and began obsessing about what was going down in Sweet Valley. I began marking the days until the book's release.

At 2:30 in the morning, on the day of its release, *Sweet Valley Confidential* downloaded to my Kindle. I spent the next three hours reading. There wasn't a page I turned, electronically speaking, where I didn't think *Girrrrrrrrl*, laugh aloud, or mutter "Mmmm." Reading this book was a vocal and emotional experience. I went to work, and when I got home, I read *Sweet Valley Confidential* again. The book was, as you might imagine, terrible, an insult to the memory of the original Sweet Valley High series. As I read, I kept thinking, *They could have called me. I work cheap.* "They," of course, have no idea who I am, but still, it hurt to know how many fans of Sweet Valley are out there, fans who could have written this book in the manner it deserved. . . .

To be fair, *Sweet Valley Confidential* could never have satisfied the expectations of those of us who fell in love with the original Sweet Valley High series. Like I said, nostalgia is powerful and the power builds with time; it often reshapes our memories. It's not that the original Sweet Valley High books were the mark of great literature, but that to some preteen and teenage girls, the books were the most familiar and resonant expressions of our angst and our fondest wishes for ourselves, the girls we wanted to become. There is a young girl-heart still throbbing in many of us. Those of us who read *Sweet Valley Confidential* were looking to recapture some of the Sweet Valley magic from our youth.

Despite the book's flaws, the magic was very much there for me. I easily embraced the drama, the absurdity, the wild implausibilities. You would not believe what's going down in Sweet Valley and who has ended up with whom, but let me tell you, it's all a delicious scandal. Someone's gay! Someone betrayed her sister. Someone's living in New York City. Someone got married to a wealthy but controlling man and lived in Europe until she escaped. Someone is engaged to be married and everyone's talking. A guy we all thought was a prince of a man is really just a man. Someone has turned into a real bitch. Someone uses baking to sublimate her sorrow. Someone had cancer. Someone became a real asshole. Someone hasn't changed one little bit. Someone got filthy rich. Someone got filthier rich. Someone died. Someone loves someone else in a tragic, unrequited way. Amidst all the drama, some things in Sweet Valley don't change. There are many happy endings. As mindless, escapist entertainment, *Sweet Valley Confidential* delivers.

I was never going to become Miss America. I know that now. Vanessa Williams and her glittering teeth could only do so much. Nonetheless, I continue to have a very active fantasy life. In one of my more elaborate, embarrassing flights of fancy, I win an Oscar for writing the Best Adapted Screenplay based on my bestselling novel, which has graced the *New York Times* bestseller list for at least fifty-seven weeks. At the Oscar ceremony I am wearing something flawless by a designer with a long, exotic name. My hair and face are beat. I don't trip when I walk up the stairs in my Louboutins to accept my honor. My date is my husband, who is the most handsome, famous movie star in the world. He is madly, uxoriously in love with me, and he beams as I stare into the audience. He will win Best Actor later in the evening because he starred in my movie. That's how we met. In my acceptance speech, I thank my parents and my agents and my famous movie-star husband and my friends. I thank Francine Pascal for creating the land of Sweet Valley and Vanessa Williams for teaching me I could be beautiful. Then I call out the names of the golden, popular kids who never loved me. I raise my Oscar over my head with one hand, and I point my fingers at a camera with the other, once again like Miss Celie laying a curse on Mister. I say, "I once told you I was going to become Miss America. This isn't the Miss America crown, but it's pretty damn close."

As a black girl, as a Haitian girl, I was not supposed to see myself in the Sweet Valley High books, but I did. Perhaps it was because I too lived in the suburbs, perhaps it was because I was looking for the way toward a perfect life and becoming Miss America, but I felt the Sweet Valley stories deeply. I read and reread the books countless times. The drama, recycled plots, and ludicrous circumstances spoke to me profoundly. This may also explain why in high school I became utterly devoted to *Beverly Hills 90210*, which took the Sweet Valley High formula and elevated it to high art. *Sweet Valley Confidential* reminded me of my most awkward years and the silly promise I made to a silly group of kids. The book reminded me of the solace, escape, and quiet joy I found in Sweet Valley. Some experiences are universal. A girl is a girl whether she lives in West Omaha or Sweet Valley. Books are often far more than just books.

The Mecca

TA-NEHISI COATES

The pursuit of knowing was freedom to me, the right to
declare your own curiosities and follow them through
all manner of books. I was made for the library, not
the classroom. Slowly, I was discovering myself.

Ta-Nehisi Coates is a national correspondent for the *Atlantic* and author
of the memoir *The Beautiful Struggle* (2008), as well as a collection of
essays, *We Were Eight Years in Power: An American Tragedy* (2017).
Coates has received the National Magazine Award, the Hillman Prize
for Opinion and Analysis Journalism, and the George Polk Award for his
Atlantic cover story "The Case for Reparations." Born in Baltimore in
1975, he currently lives in New York.

In this excerpt from his groundbreaking 2015 work, *Between the
World and Me*, that imparts his questions, concerns, and ideals in
the form of a letter to his son, Ta-Nehisi Coates offers a look at how
the renowned research center at historically Black Howard University
awakened in him the freedom to explore revelations of his own history
and identity.

S on,
        ... I was admitted to Howard University, but formed and shaped by The Mecca. These institutions are related but not the same. Howard University is an institution of higher education, concerned with the LSAT, magna cum laude, and Phi Beta Kappa. The Mecca is a machine, crafted to capture and concentrate the dark energy of all African peoples and inject it directly into the student body. The Mecca derives its power from the heritage of Howard University, which in Jim Crow days enjoyed a near-monopoly on black talent. And whereas most other historically black schools were scattered like forts in the great wilderness of the old Confederacy, Howard was in Washington, D.C.—Chocolate City—and thus in proximity to both federal power and black power. The result was an alumni and professoriat that spanned genre and generation—Charles Drew, Amiri Baraka, Thurgood Marshall, Ossie Davis, Doug Wilder, David Dinkins, Lucille Clifton, Toni Morrison, Kwame Ture. The history, the location, the alumni combined to create The Mecca—the crossroads of the black diaspora.

I first witnessed this power out on the Yard, that communal green space in the center of the campus where the students gathered and I saw everything I knew of my black self multiplied out into seemingly endless variations. There were the scions of Nigerian aristocrats in their business suits giving dap to bald-headed Qs in purple windbreakers and tan Timbs. There were the high-yellow progeny of AME preachers debating the clerics of Ausar-Set. There were California girls turned Muslims, born anew, in hijab and long skirt. There were Ponzi schemers and Christian cultists, Tabernacle fanatics and mathematical geniuses. It was like listening to a hundred different renditions of "Redemption Song," each in a different color and key. And overlaying all of this was the history of Howard itself. I knew that I was literally walking in the footsteps of all the Toni Morrisons, and Zora Neale Hurstons, of all the Sterling Browns and Kenneth Clarks, who'd come before. The Mecca—the vastness of black people across space-time—could be experienced in a twenty-minute walk across campus. I saw this vastness in the students chopping it up in front of the Frederick Douglass Memorial Hall, where Muhammad Ali had addressed their fathers and mothers in defiance of the Vietnam War. I saw its epic sweep in the students next to Ira Aldridge Theater, where Donny Hathaway had once sung, where Donald Byrd had once assembled his flock. The students came out with their saxophones, trumpets, and drums, played "My Favorite Things" or "Someday My Prince Will Come." Some of the other students were out on the grass in front of Alain Locke Hall, in pink and green, chanting, singing, stomping, clapping, stepping. Some of them came up from Tubman Quadrangle with their roommates and rope for Double Dutch. Some of them came down from Drew Hall, with their caps cocked and their backpacks slung through one arm, then fell into gorgeous ciphers of beatbox and rhyme. Some of the girls sat by the flagpole with bell hooks and Sonia Sanchez in their straw totes. Some of the boys, with their new Yoruba names, beseeched these girls by citing Frantz Fanon. Some of them studied Russian. Some of them worked in bone labs. They were Panamanian. They were Bajan. And some of them were from places I had never heard of. But all of them were hot and incredible, exotic even, though we hailed from the same tribe.

The black world was expanding before me, and I could see now that that world was more than a photonegative of that of the people who believe they are white. "White America" is a syndicate arrayed to protect its exclusive power to dominate and control our bodies. Sometimes this power is direct (lynching), and sometimes it is insidious (redlining). But however it appears, the power of domination and exclusion is central to the belief in being white, and without it, "white people" would cease to exist for want of reasons. There will surely always be people with straight hair and blue eyes, as there have been for all history. But some of these straight-haired people with blue eyes have been "black," and this points to the great difference between their world and ours. We did not choose our fences. They were imposed on us by Virginia planters obsessed with enslaving as many Americans as possible. They are the ones who came up with a one-drop rule that separated the "white" from the "black," even if it meant that their own blue-eyed sons would live under the lash. The result is a people, black people, who embody all physical varieties and whose life stories mirror this physical range. Through The Mecca I saw that we were, in our own segregated body politic, cosmopolitans. The black diaspora was not just our own world but, in so many ways, the Western world itself.

Now, the heirs of those Virginia planters could never directly acknowledge this legacy or reckon with its power. And so that beauty that Malcolm pledged us to protect, black beauty, was never celebrated in movies, in television, or in the textbooks I'd seen as a child. Everyone of any import, from Jesus to George Washington, was white. This was why your grandparents banned Tarzan and the Lone Ranger and toys with white faces from the house. They were rebelling against the history books that spoke of black people only as sentimental "firsts"—first black five-star general, first black congressman, first black mayor—always presented in the bemused manner of a category of Trivial Pursuit. Serious history was the West, and the West was white. This was all distilled for me in a quote I once read from the novelist Saul Bellow. I can't remember where I read it, or when—only that I was already at Howard. "Who is the Tolstoy of the Zulus?" Bellow quipped. Tolstoy was "white," and so Tolstoy "mattered," like everything else that was white "mattered." And this view of things was connected to the fear that passed through the generations, to the sense of dispossession. We were black, beyond the visible spectrum, beyond civilization. Our history was inferior because we were inferior, which is to say our bodies were inferior. And our inferior bodies could not possibly be accorded the same respect as those that built the West. Would it not be better, then, if our bodies were civilized, improved, and put to some legitimate Christian use?

Contrary to this theory, I had Malcolm. I had my mother and father. I had my readings of every issue of *The Source* and *Vibe*. I read them not merely because I loved black music—I did—but because of the writing itself. Writers Greg Tate, Chairman Mao, dream hampton—barely older than me—were out there creating a new language, one that I intuitively understood, to analyze our art, our world. This was, in and of itself, an argument for the weight and beauty of our culture and thus of our bodies. And now each day, out on the Yard, I felt this weight and saw this beauty, not just as a matter of theory but also as a demonstrable fact. And I wanted desperately to communicate this evidence to the world, because I felt—even if I did not completely know—that the larger culture's erasure of black beauty was intimately connected to the destruction of black bodies.

What was required was a new story, a new history told through the lens of our struggle. I had always known this, had heard the need for a new history in Malcolm, had seen the need addressed in my father's books. It was in the promise behind their grand titles— *Children of the Sun*, *Wonderful Ethiopians of the Ancient Cushite Empire*, *The African Origin of Civilization*. Here was not just our history but the history of the world, weaponized to our noble ends. Here was the primordial stuff of our own Dream—the Dream of a "black race"—of our own Tolstoys who lived deep in the African past, where we authored operas, pioneered secret algebra, erected ornate walls, pyramids, colossi, bridges, roads, and all the inventions that I then thought must qualify one's lineage for the ranks of civilization. They had their champions, and somewhere we must have ours. By then I'd read Chancellor Williams, J. A. Rogers, and John Jackson— writers central to the canon of our new noble history. From them I knew that Mansa Musa of Mali was black, and Shabaka of Egypt was black, and Yaa Asantewaa of Ashanti was black—and "the black race" was a thing I supposed existed from time immemorial, a thing that was real and mattered.

When I came to Howard, Chancellor Williams's *Destruction of Black Civilization* was my Bible. Williams himself had taught at Howard. I read him when I was sixteen, and his work offered a grand theory of multi-millennial European plunder. The theory relieved me of certain troubling questions—this is the point of nationalism—and it gave me my Tolstoy. I read about Queen Nzinga, who ruled in Central Africa in the sixteenth century, resisting the Portuguese. I read about her negotiating with the Dutch. When the Dutch ambassador tried to humiliate her by refusing her a seat, Nzinga had shown her power by ordering one of her advisers to all fours to make a human chair of her body. That was the kind of power I sought, and the story of our own royalty became for me a weapon. My working theory then held all black people as kings in exile, a nation of original men severed from our original names and our majestic Nubian culture. Surely this was the message I took from gazing out in the Yard. Had any people, anywhere, ever been as sprawling and beautiful as us?

I needed more books. At Howard University, one of the greatest collections of books could be found in the Moorland-Spingarn Research Center, where your grandfather once worked. Moorland held archives, papers, collections, and virtually any book ever written by or about black people. For the most significant portion of my time at The Mecca, I followed a simple ritual. I would walk into the Moorland reading room and fill out three call slips for three different works. I would take a seat at one of these long tables. I would draw out my pen and one of my black-and-white composition books. I would open the books and read, while filling my composition books with notes on my reading, new vocabulary words, and sentences of my own invention. I would arrive in the morning and request, three call slips at a time, the works of every writer I had heard spoken of in classrooms or out on the Yard: Larry Neal, Eric Williams, George Padmore, Sonia Sanchez, Stanley Crouch, Harold Cruse, Manning Marable, Addison Gayle, Carolyn Rodgers, Etheridge Knight, Sterling Brown. I remember believing that the key to all life lay in articulating the precise difference between "the Black Aesthetic" and "Negritude." How, specifically, did Europe underdevelop Africa? I must know. And if the Eighteenth Dynasty pharaohs were alive today, would they live in Harlem? I had to inhale all the pages.

I went into this investigation imagining history to be a unified narrative, free of debate, which, once uncovered, would simply verify everything I had always suspected. The smokescreen would lift. And the villains who manipulated the schools and the streets would be unmasked. But there was so much to know—so much geography to cover—Africa, the Caribbean, the Americas, the United States. And all of these areas had histories, sprawling literary canons, fieldwork, ethnographies. Where should I begin?

The trouble came almost immediately. I did not find a coherent tradition marching lockstep but instead factions, and factions within factions. Hurston battled Hughes, Du Bois warred with Garvey, Harold Cruse fought everyone. I felt myself at the bridge of a great ship that I could not control because C. L. R. James was a great wave and Basil Davidson was a swirling eddy, tossing me about. Things I believed merely a week earlier, ideas I had taken from one book, could be smashed to splinters by another. Had we retained any of our African inheritance? Frazier says it was all destroyed, and this destruction evidences the terribleness of our capturers. Herskovitz says it lives on, and this evidences the resilience of our African spirit. By my second year, it was natural for me to spend a typical day mediating between Frederick Douglass's integration into America and Martin Delany's escape into nationalism. Perhaps they were somehow both right. I had come looking for a parade, for a military review of champions marching in ranks. Instead I was left with a brawl of ancestors, a herd of dissenters, sometimes marching together but just as often marching away from each other.

I would take breaks from my reading, walk out to the vendors who lined the streets, eat lunch on the Yard. I would imagine Malcolm, his body bound in a cell, studying the books, trading his human eyes for the power of flight. And I too felt bound by my ignorance, by the questions that I had not yet understood to be more than just means, by my lack of understanding, and by Howard itself. It was still a school, after all. I wanted to pursue things, to know things, but I could not match the means of knowing that came naturally to me with the expectations of professors. The pursuit of knowing was freedom to me, the right to declare your own curiosities and follow them through all manner of books. I was made for the library, not the classroom. The classroom was a jail of other people's interests. The library was open, unending, free. Slowly, I was discovering myself. The best parts of Malcolm pointed the way. Malcolm, always changing, always evolving toward some truth that was ultimately outside the boundaries of his life, of his body. I felt myself in motion, still directed toward the total possession of my body, but by some other route which I could not before then have imagined.

The Danger of the Single Story

CHIMAMANDA NGOZI ADICHIE

> Stories matter. Many stories matter. Stories have
> been used to dispossess and to malign, but stories
> can also be used to empower and to humanize.

Chimamanda Ngozi Adichie, born in 1977, grew up in Nigeria. She is the author of the novels *Purple Hibiscus*, which won the Commonwealth Writers' Prize and the Hurston/Wright Legacy Award, and *Half of a Yellow Sun*, which won the Orange Prize and was a National Book Critics Circle Award Finalist, a *New York Times Notable Book*, and a *People* and *Black Issues Book Review* Best Book of the Year; and the story collection *The Thing Around Your Neck*. Her novel *Americanah*, published in 2013, received numerous accolades, including the National Book Critics Circle Award for Fiction and the Chicago Tribune Heartland Prize for Fiction, and was named one of the *New York Times Ten Best Books of the Year*. A recipient of a MacArthur Foundation Fellowship, Adichie divides her time between the United States and Nigeria.

Adichie's speech for TEDxEuston in 2012 entitled "We Should All Be Feminists" was sampled for the 2013 song "Flawless" by American entertainer Beyoncé. Adichie's first TED Talk, in 2009, "The Danger of a Single Story," which discusses how perceptions of people globally are formed by literature, drew great attention and is presented here.

'm a storyteller. And I would like to tell you a few personal stories about what I like to call "the danger of the single story." I grew up on a university campus in eastern Nigeria. My mother says that I started reading at the age of two, although I think four is probably close to the truth. So I was an early reader, and what I read were British and American children's books.

I was also an early writer, and when I began to write, at about the age of seven, stories in pencil with crayon illustrations that my poor mother was obligated to read, I wrote exactly the kinds of stories I was reading: All my characters were white and blue-eyed, they played in the snow, they ate apples, and they talked a lot about the weather, how lovely it was that the sun had come out. Now, this despite the fact that I lived in Nigeria. I had never been outside Nigeria. We didn't have snow, we ate mangoes, and we never talked about the weather, because there was no need to.

My characters also drank a lot of ginger beer because the characters in the British books I read drank ginger beer. Never mind that I had no idea what ginger beer was. And for many years afterwards, I would have a desperate desire to taste ginger beer. But that is another story.

What this demonstrates, I think, is how impressionable and vulnerable we are in the face of a story, particularly as children. Because all I had read were books in which characters were foreign, I had become convinced that books by their very nature had to have foreigners in them and had to be about things with which I could not personally identify. Things changed when I discovered African books. There weren't many of them available, and they weren't quite as easy to find as the foreign books.

But because of writers like Chinua Achebe and Camara Laye, I went through a mental shift in my perception of literature. I realized that people like me, girls with skin the color of chocolate, whose kinky hair could not form ponytails, could also exist in literature. I started to write about things I recognized.

Now, I loved those American and British books I read. They stirred my imagination. They opened up new worlds for me. But the unintended consequence was that I did not know that people like me could exist in literature. So what the discovery of African writers did for me was this: It saved me from having a single story of what books are.

I come from a conventional, middle-class Nigerian family. My father was a professor. My mother was an administrator. And so we had, as was the norm, live-in domestic help, who would often come from nearby rural villages. So the year I turned eight we got a new house boy. His name was Fide. The only thing my mother told us about him was that his family was very poor. My mother sent yams and rice, and our old clothes, to his family. And when I didn't finish my dinner my mother would say, "Finish your food! Don't you know? People like Fide's family have nothing." So I felt enormous pity for Fide's family.

Then one Saturday we went to his village to visit, and his mother showed us a beautifully patterned basket made of dyed raffia that his brother had made. I was startled. It had not occurred to me that anybody in his family could actually make something. All I had heard about them was how poor they were, so that it had become impossible for me to see them as anything else but poor. Their poverty was my single story of them.

Years later, I thought about this when I left Nigeria to go to university in the United States. I was 19. My American roommate was shocked by me. She asked where I had learned to speak English so well, and was confused when I said that Nigeria happened to have English as its official language. She asked if she could listen to what she called my "tribal music," and was consequently very disappointed when I produced my tape of Mariah Carey. She assumed that I did not know how to use a stove.

What struck me was this: She had felt sorry for me even before she saw me. Her default position toward me, as an African, was a kind of patronizing, well-meaning pity. My roommate had a single story of Africa: a single story of catastrophe. In this single story there was no possibility of Africans being similar to her in any way, no possibility of feelings more complex than pity, no possibility of a connection as human equals.

I must say that before I went to the US I didn't consciously identify as African. But in the US whenever Africa came up people turned to me. Never mind that I knew nothing about places like Namibia. But I did come to embrace this new identity, and in many ways I think of myself now as African. Although I still get quite irritable when Africa is referred to as a country, the most recent example being my otherwise wonderful flight from Lagos two days ago, in which there was an announcement on the Virgin flight about the charity work in "India, Africa and other countries."

So after I had spent some years in the US as an African, I began to understand my roommate's response to me. If I had not grown up in Nigeria, and if all I knew about Africa were from popular images, I too would think that Africa was a place of beautiful landscapes, beautiful animals, and incomprehensible people, fighting senseless wars, dying of poverty and AIDS, unable to speak for themselves, and waiting to be saved by a kind, white foreigner. I would see Africans in the same way that I, as a child, had seen Fide's family.

This single story of Africa ultimately comes, I think, from Western literature. Now, here is a quote from the writing of a London merchant called John Locke, who sailed to West Africa in 1561 and kept a fascinating account of his voyage. After referring to the black Africans as "beasts who have no houses," he writes, "They are also people without heads, having their mouth and eyes in their breasts."

Now, I've laughed every time I've read this. And one must admire the imagination of John Locke. But what is important about his writing is that it represents the beginning of a tradition of telling African stories in the West: a tradition of Sub-Saharan Africa as a place of negatives, of difference, of darkness, of people who, in the words of the wonderful poet Rudyard Kipling, are "half devil, half child."

And so I began to realize that my American roommate must have throughout her life seen and heard different versions of this single story, as had a professor, who once told me that my novel was not "authentically African." Now, I was quite willing to contend that there were a number of things wrong with the novel, that it had failed in a number of places, but I had not quite imagined that it had failed at achieving something called African authenticity. In fact I did not know what African authenticity was. The professor told me that my characters were too much like him, an educated and middle-class man. My characters drove cars. They were not starving. Therefore they were not authentically African.

But I must quickly add that I too am just as guilty in the question of the single story. A few years ago, I visited Mexico from the US. The political climate in the US at the time was tense, and there were debates going on about immigration. And, as often happens in America, immigration became synonymous with Mexicans. There were endless stories of Mexicans as people who were fleecing the health-care system, sneaking across the border, being arrested at the border, that sort of thing.

I remember walking around on my first day in Guadalajara, watching the people going to work, rolling up tortillas in the marketplace, smoking, laughing. I remember first feeling slight surprise. And then I was overwhelmed with shame. I realized that I had been so immersed in the media coverage of Mexicans that they had become one thing in my mind, the abject immigrant. I had bought into the single story of Mexicans and I could not have been more ashamed of myself. So that is how to create a single story, show a people as one thing, as only one thing, over and over again, and that is what they become.

It is impossible to talk about the single story without talking about power. There is a word, an Igbo word that I think about whenever I think about the power structures of the world, and it is "nkali." It's a noun that loosely translates to "to be greater than another." Like our economic and political worlds, stories too are defined by the principle of nkali: How they are told, who tells them, when they're told, how many stories are told, are really dependent on power.

Power is the ability not just to tell the story of another person, but to make it the definitive story of that person. The Palestinian

poet Mourid Barghouti writes that if you want to dispossess a people, the simplest way to do it is to tell their story and to start with,
"secondly." Start the story with the arrows of the Native Americans,
and not with the arrival of the British, and you have an entirely different story. Start the story with the failure of the African state, and
not with the colonial creation of the African state, and you have an
entirely different story.

I recently spoke at a university where a student told me that it
was such a shame that Nigerian men were physical abusers like the
father character in my novel. I told him that I had just read a novel
called *American Psycho*—and that it was such a shame that young
Americans were serial murderers. Now, obviously I said this in a fit
of mild irritation. But it would never have occurred to me to think
that just because I had read a novel in which a character was a serial
killer that he was somehow representative of all Americans. This is
not because I am a better person than that student, but because of
America's cultural and economic power, I had many stories of America. I had read Tyler and Updike and Steinbeck and Gaitskill. I did
not have a single story of America.

When I learned, some years ago, that writers were expected to
have had really unhappy childhoods to be successful, I began to
think about how I could invent horrible things my parents had done
to me. But the truth is that I had a very happy childhood, full of
laughter and love, in a very close-knit family.

But I also had grandfathers who died in refugee camps. My
cousin Polle died because he could not get adequate health care. One
of my closest friends, Okoloma, died in a plane crash because our
fire trucks did not have water. I grew up under repressive military
governments that devalued education, so that sometimes my parents
were not paid their salaries. And so, as a child, I saw jam disappear
from the breakfast table, then margarine disappeared, then bread
became too expensive, then milk became rationed. And most of all,
a kind of normalized political fear invaded our lives.

All of these stories make me who I am. But to insist on only these
negative stories is to flatten my experience and to overlook the many

other stories that formed me. The single story creates stereotypes, and the problem with stereotypes is not that they are untrue, but that they are incomplete. They make one story become the only story.

Of course, Africa is a continent full of catastrophes: There are immense ones, such as the horrific rapes in Congo and depressing ones, such as the fact that five thousand people apply for one job vacancy in Nigeria. But there are other stories that are not about catastrophe, and it is very important, it is just as important, to talk about them.

I've always felt that it is impossible to engage properly with a place or a person without engaging with all of the stories of that place and that person. The consequence of the single story is this: It robs people of dignity. It makes our recognition of our equal humanity difficult. It emphasizes how we are different rather than how we are similar.

So what if before my Mexican trip I had followed the immigration debate from both sides, the US and the Mexican? What if my mother had told us that Fide's family was poor and hardworking? What if we had an African television network that broadcast diverse African stories all over the world? What the Nigerian writer Chinua Achebe calls "a balance of stories."

What if my roommate knew about my Nigerian publisher, Mukta Bakaray, a remarkable man who left his job in a bank to follow his dream and start a publishing house? Now, the conventional wisdom was that Nigerians don't read literature. He disagreed. He felt that people who could read, would read, if you made literature affordable and available to them.

Shortly after he published my first novel I went to a TV station in Lagos to do an interview, and a woman who worked there as a messenger came up to me and said, "I really liked your novel. I didn't like the ending. Now you must write a sequel, and this is what will happen . . ." And she went on to tell me what to write in the sequel. I was not only charmed, I was very moved. Here was a woman, part of the ordinary masses of Nigerians, who were not supposed to be readers. She had not only read the book, but she had taken ownership of it and felt justified in telling me what to write in the sequel.

Now, what if my roommate knew about my friend Fumi Onda, a fearless woman who hosts a TV show in Lagos, and is determined to tell the stories that we prefer to forget? What if my roommate knew about the heart procedure that was performed in the Lagos hospital last week? What if my roommate knew about contemporary Nigerian music, talented people singing in English and Pidgin, and Igbo and Yoruba and Ijo, mixing influences from Jay Z to Fela to Bob Marley to their grandfathers. What if my roommate knew about the female lawyer who recently went to court in Nigeria to challenge a ridiculous law that required women to get their husband's consent before renewing their passports? What if my roommate knew about Nollywood, full of innovative people making films despite great technical odds, films so popular that they really are the best example of Nigerians consuming what they produce? What if my roommate knew about my wonderfully ambitious hair braider, who has just started her own business selling hair extensions? Or about the millions of other Nigerians who start businesses and sometimes fail, but continue to nurse ambition?

Every time I am home I am confronted with the usual sources of irritation for most Nigerians: our failed infrastructure, our failed government, but also by the incredible resilience of people who thrive despite the government, rather than because of it. I teach writing workshops in Lagos every summer, and it is amazing to me how many people apply, how many people are eager to write, to tell stories.

My Nigerian publisher and I have just started a nonprofit called Farafina Trust, and we have big dreams of building libraries and refurbishing libraries that already exist and providing books for state schools that don't have anything in their libraries, and also of organizing lots and lots of workshops, in reading and writing, for all the people who are eager to tell our many stories. Stories matter. Many stories matter. Stories have been used to dispossess and to malign, but stories can also be used to empower and to humanize. Stories can break the dignity of a people, but stories can also repair that broken dignity.

The American writer Alice Walker wrote this about her Southern relatives who had moved to the North. She introduced them to a book about the Southern life that they had left behind: "They sat around, reading the book themselves, listening to me read the book, and a kind of paradise was regained."

I would like to end with this thought: That when we reject the single story, when we realize that there is never a single story about any place, we regain a kind of paradise.

What Books Mean to Me

AN INTERVIEW WITH PRESIDENT BARACK OBAMA

In my post-presidency, in addition to training the next generation of leaders to work on issues like climate change or gun violence or criminal justice reform, my hope is to link them up with their peers who see fiction or nonfiction as an important part of that process.

With a father from Kenya and a mother from Kansas, Barack Hussein Obama was born in Honolulu, Hawaii, in 1961. Raised with the help of his grandparents, he worked his way through college (Occidental College and Columbia University) and went on to attend Harvard Law School, where he became the first African American president of the *Harvard Law Review*. Upon graduation, he relocated to Chicago to help lead a voter registration drive, teach constitutional law at the University of Chicago Law School, and eventually become a United States senator. He was elected the 44th President of the United States on November 4, 2008, and was reelected in 2012, serving until the end of his term on January 20, 2017. Still making a difference, he and the former First Lady Michelle Obama have established the Obama Foundation, while writing their memoirs and as planning takes place for the Obama Presidential Library.

This interview with President Obama by Michiko Kakutani, formerly the *New York Times*'s chief book critic, appeared in the *Times* on January 16, 2017, as his days in the White House were winding down. What the interview has in common with the other first-person narratives of this anthology is that it allowed the president to speak directly to the reader in his own voice. Here he discusses his lifelong love of reading and writing, from his childhood to his college days and time as a community activist, and through his eight historic and glorious years as President of the United States of America.

What made you want to become a writer?

I loved reading when I was a kid, partly because I was traveling so much, and there were times where I'd be displaced, I'd be the outsider. When I first moved to Indonesia, I'm this big, dark-skinned kid that kind of stood out. And then when I moved back from Indonesia to Hawaii, I had the manners and habits probably of an Indonesian kid.

And so the idea of having these worlds that were portable, that were yours, that you could enter into, was appealing to me. And then I became a teenager and wasn't reading that much other than what was assigned in school, and playing basketball and chasing girls, and imbibing things that weren't very healthy.

I think all of us did.

Yeah. And then I think I rediscovered writing and reading and thinking in my first or second year of college and used that as a way to rebuild myself, a process I write about in *Dreams from My Father*.

That period in New York, where you were intensely reading.

I was hermetic—it really is true. I had one plate, one towel, and I'd buy clothes from thrift shops. And I was very intense, and sort of humorless. But it reintroduced me to the power of words as a way to figure out who you are and what you think, and what you believe, and what's important, and to sort through and interpret this swirl of events that is happening around you every minute.

And so even though by the time I graduated I knew I wanted to be involved in public policy, or I had these vague notions of organizing, the idea of continuing to write and tell stories as part of that was valuable to me. And so I would come home from work, and I would write in my journal or write a story or two.

The great thing was that it was useful in my organizing work. Because when I got there, the guy who had hired me said that the thing that brings people together to have the courage to take action on behalf of their lives is not just that they care about the same issue, it's that they have shared stories. And he told me that if you learn how to listen to people's stories and can find what's sacred in other people's stories, then you'll be able to forge a relationship that lasts.

But my interest in public service and politics then merged with the idea of storytelling.

What were your short stories like?

It's interesting, when I read them, a lot of them had to do with older people.

I think part of the reason was because I was working in communities with people who were significantly older than me. We were going into churches, and probably the average age of these folks was 55, 60. A lot of them had scratched and clawed their way into the middle class, but just barely. They were seeing the communities in which they had invested their hopes and dreams and raised their kids starting to decay—steel mills had closed, and there had been a lot of racial turnover in these communities. And so there was also this sense of loss and disappointment.

And so a bunch of the short stories I wrote had to do with that sense, that atmosphere. One story is about an old black pastor who seems to be about to lose his church, his lease is running out and he's got this loyal woman deacon who is trying to buck him up. Another is about an elderly couple—a white couple in L.A.—and he's like in advertising, wrote jingles. And he's just retired and has gotten cranky. And his wife is trying to convince him that his life is not over.

So when I think back on what's interesting to me, there is not a lot of Jack Kerouac, open-road, young kid on the make discovering stuff. It's more melancholy and reflective.

Was writing partly a way to figure out your identity?

Yes, I think so. For me, particularly at that time, writing was the way I sorted through a lot of crosscurrents in my life—race, class, family. And I genuinely believe that it was part of the way in which

I was able to integrate all these pieces of myself into something relatively whole.

People now remark on this notion of me being very cool, or composed. And what is true is that I generally have a pretty good sense of place and who I am, and what's important to me. And I trace a lot of that back to that process of writing.

Has that continued to be so in the presidency?

Not as much as I would have liked. I just didn't have time.

But you keep some form of a journal?

I've kept some, but not with the sort of discipline that I would have hoped for. The main writing that I've done during the presidency has been my speeches, the ones at least that were important to me.

How has the speechwriting and being at the center of history and dealing with crises affected you as a writer?

I'm not sure yet. I'll have to see when I start writing the next book. Some of the craft of writing a good speech is identical to any other good writing: Is that word necessary? Is it the right word? Is there a rhythm to it that feels good? How does it sound aloud?

I actually think that one of the useful things about speechwriting is reminding yourself that the original words are spoken, and that there is a sound, a feel to words that, even if you're reading silently, transmits itself.

So in that sense, I think there will be some consistency.

But this is part of why it was important to pick up the occasional novel during the presidency, because most of my reading every day was briefing books and memos and proposals. And so working that very analytical side of the brain all the time sometimes meant you lost track of not just the poetry of fiction, but also the depth of fiction.

Fiction was useful as a reminder of the truths under the surface of what we argue about every day and was a way of seeing and hearing the voices, the multitudes of this country.

Are there examples of specific novels or writers?

Well, the last novel I read was Colson Whitehead's *The Underground Railroad.* And the reminder of the ways in which the pain of slavery transmits itself across generations, not just in overt ways, but how it changes minds and hearts.

It's what you said in your farewell address about Atticus Finch, where you said people are so isolated in their little bubbles. Fiction can leap—

It bridges them. I struck up a friendship with [the novelist] Marilynne Robinson, who has become a good friend. And we've become sort of pen pals. I started reading her in Iowa, where *Gilead* and some of her best novels are set. And I loved her writing in part because I saw those people every day. And the interior life she was describing that connected them—the people I was shaking hands with and making speeches to—it connected them with my grandparents, who were from Kansas and ended up journeying all the way to Hawaii, but whose foundation had been set in a very similar setting.

And so I think that I found myself better able to imagine what's going on in the lives of people throughout my presidency because of not just a specific novel but the act of reading fiction. It exercises those muscles, and I think that has been helpful.

And then there's been the occasion where I just want to get out of my own head. [Laughter] Sometimes you read fiction just because you want to be someplace else.

What are some of those books?

It's interesting, the stuff I read just to escape ends up being a mix of things—some science fiction. For a while, there was a three-volume science-fiction novel, the "Three-Body Problem" series—

Oh, Liu Cixin, who won the Hugo Award.

—which was just wildly imaginative, really interesting. It wasn't so much sort of character studies as it was just this sweeping—

It's really about the fate of the universe.

Exactly. The scope of it was immense. So that was fun to read, partly because my day-to-day problems with Congress seem fairly petty—not something to worry about. Aliens are about to invade. [Laughter]

There were books that would blend, I think, really good writing with thriller genres. I mean, I thought *Gone Girl* was a well-constructed, well-written book.

I loved that structure.

Yeah, and it was really well executed. And a similar structure, that I thought was a really powerful novel: *Fates and Furies*, by Lauren Groff.

I like those structures where you actually see different points of view.

Which I have to do for this job, too. [Laughter]

Have there been certain books that have been touchstones for you in these eight years?

I would say Shakespeare continues to be a touchstone. Like most teenagers in high school, when we were assigned, I don't know, *The Tempest* or something, I thought, "My God, this is boring." And I took this wonderful Shakespeare class in college where I just started to read the tragedies and dig into them. And that, I think, is foundational for me in understanding how certain patterns repeat themselves and play themselves out between human beings.

Is that sort of comforting?

It gives me a sense of perspective. I think Toni Morrison's writings—particularly *Song of Solomon* is a book I think of when I imagine people going through hardship. That it's not just pain, but there's joy and glory and mystery.

I think that there are writers who I don't necessarily agree with in terms of their politics, but whose writings are sort of a baseline for how to think about certain things—V. S. Naipaul, for example. His *A Bend in the River*, which starts with the line, "The world is what it is; men who are nothing, who allow themselves to become nothing, have no place in it." And I always think about that line, and I think about his novels when I'm thinking about the hardness of the world sometimes, particularly in foreign policy, and I resist and fight against sometimes that very cynical, more realistic view of the world. And yet, there are times where it feels as if that may be true.

So in that sense, I'm using writing like that as a foil or something to debate against.

I've read that Lincoln loved Shakespeare his whole life, but when he was dealing with the Civil War, reading the history plays helped give him solace and perspective.

Lincoln's own writings do that. He is a very fine writer.

I'd put the Second Inaugural up against any piece of American writing—as good as anything. One of the great treats of being president is, in the Lincoln Bedroom, there's a copy of the Gettysburg Address handwritten by him, one of five copies he did for charity. And there have been times in the evening when I'd just walk over, because it's right next to my office, my home office, and I just read it.

And perspective is exactly what is wanted. At a time when events move so quickly and so much information is transmitted, the ability to slow down and get perspective, along with the ability to get in somebody else's shoes—those two things have been invaluable to me. Whether they've made me a better president, I can't say. But what I can say is that they have allowed me to sort of maintain my balance during the course of eight years, because this is a place that comes at you hard and fast and doesn't let up.

Is there some poem or any writing or author that you would turn to, say, after the mass killings in Newtown, Conn., or during the financial crisis?

I think that during those periods, Lincoln's writings, King's writings, Gandhi's writings, Mandela's writings—I found those particularly helpful, because what you wanted was a sense of solidarity. During very difficult moments, this job can be very isolating. So sometimes you have to hop across history to find folks who have been similarly feeling isolated. Churchill's a good writer. And I loved reading Teddy Roosevelt's writing. He's this big, outsize character.

Have you read a lot of presidential biographies?

The biographies have been useful, because I do think that there's a tendency, understandable, to think that whatever's going on right now is uniquely disastrous or amazing or difficult. And it just serves you well to think about Roosevelt trying to navigate World War II or Lincoln trying to figure out whether he's going to fire [George B.] McClellan when Rebel troops are 20, 30, 40 miles away.

I watched some of the civil-rights-movement documentary miniseries *Eyes on the Prize* after the election.

It was useful.

You do see how far we've come, and in the space of my lifetime.

And that's why seeing my daughters now picking up books that I read 30 years ago or 40 years ago is gratifying, because I want them to have perspective—not for purposes of complacency, but rather to give them confidence that people with a sense of determination and courage and pluck can reshape things. It's empowering for them.

What books would you recommend at this moment in time, that capture this sense of turmoil?

I should probably ask you or some people who have had time to catch up on reading. I'll confess that since the election, I've been busier than I expected. So one of the things I'm really looking forward to is to dig into a whole bunch of literature.

But one of the things I'm confident about is that, out of this moment, there are a whole bunch of writers, a lot of them young, who are probably writing the book I need to read. [Laughter] They're ahead of me right now. And so in my post-presidency, in addition to training the next generation of leaders to work on issues like climate change or gun violence or criminal justice reform, my hope is to link them up with their peers who see fiction or nonfiction as an important part of that process.

When so much of our politics is trying to manage this clash of cultures brought about by globalization and technology and migration, the role of stories to unify—as opposed to divide, to engage rather than to marginalize—is more important than ever.

There's something particular about quieting yourself and having a sustained stretch of time that is different from music or television or even the greatest movies.

And part of what we're all having to deal with right now is just a lot of information overload and a lack of time to process things. So we make quick judgments and assign stereotypes to things, block certain things out, because our brain is just trying to get through the day.

We're bombarded with information. Technology is moving so rapidly.

Look, I don't worry about the survival of the novel. We're a storytelling species.

I think that what one of the jobs of political leaders going forward is, is to tell a better story about what binds us together as a people. And America is unique in having to stitch together all these disparate elements—we're not one race, we're not one tribe, folks didn't all arrive here at the same time.

What holds us together is an idea, and it's a story about who we are and what's important to us. And I want to make sure that we continue that.

I know you like Junot Díaz's and Jhumpa Lahiri's books, and they speak to immigration or the American Dream.

I think Lahiri's books, I think Díaz's books, do speak to a very particular contemporary immigration experience. But also this combination of—that I think is universal—longing for this better place, but also feeling displaced and looking backwards at the same time. I think in that sense, their novels are directly connected to a lot of American literature.

Some of the great books by Jewish authors like Philip Roth or Saul Bellow, they are steeped with this sense of being an outsider, longing to get in, not sure what you're giving up—what you're willing to give up and what you're not willing to give up. So that particular aspect of American fiction I think is still of great relevance today.

PERMISSIONS AND CREDITS

FOREWORD

"Our First Stories": by Nikki Giovanni. Copyright © 2018 by Nikki Giovanni. Original essay for *Black Ink* published in arrangement with and by permission of Nikki Giovanni. All rights reserved.

INTRODUCTION

"Reading Matters": an original essay by the editor of *Black Ink*. Copyright © 2018 by Stephanie Stokes Oliver.

ESSAYS

"Suspected of Having a Book": *Narrative of the Life of Frederick Douglass, an American Slave, Written by Himself.* Originally published in 1845. This excerpt from the edition published by Open Media Series, City Lights Books, 2010. Subtitle: *A New Critical Edition by Angela Y. Davis, Featuring Her "Lectures On Liberation."*

"Nine Years Deprived of a Sheet of Paper": from Penguin Classics edition of *Twelve Years a Slave* by Solomon Northup, Penguin Books, 2012. Originally published by Derby and Miller, 1853.

"A Whole Race Begins to Read": *Up from Slavery* by Booker T. Washington. Originally published by Doubleday, Page and Company, 1901. Dover Thrift Edition copyright © 1995 by Dover Publications.

"The Negro in Literature and Art": *W. E. B. Du Bois: Writings*, edited by Nathan Huggins. Copyright © 1986 by Literary Classics of the United States, Inc., New York, NY. All rights reserved. Adapted from Essays and Articles section: "The Negro in Literature and Art," originally published in the *Annals of the American Academy of Political and Social Science*, September 1913; and "Criteria of Negro Art," the text of an address delivered at the Chicago Conference of the NAACP in 1926, and published in *The Crisis*, October 1926.

the United States. The printing, copying, redistribution, or retransmission of the Content without express written permission is prohibited.

"Reading for Revolution" from: *Ready for Revolution: The Life and Struggles of Stokely Carmichael (Kwame Ture)* by Stokely Carmichael (Kwame Ture) with Ekwueme Michael Thelwell. Copyright © 2003 by Kwame Ture and Ekwueme Michael Thelwell. Reprinted with the permission of Scribner, a division of Simon & Schuster, Inc. All rights reserved.

"Twenty-One": excerpt from "From an Interview" from *In Search of Our Mothers' Gardens: Womanist Prose* by Alice Walker. Copyright © 1973 by Alice Walker. Reprinted by permission of Houghton Mifflin Harcourt Publishing Company; and by permission of The Joy Harris Literary Agency, Inc. All rights reserved.

"A Temporary Library in a Small Place": from *A Small Place* by Jamaica Kincaid. Copyright © 1988 by Jamaica Kincaid. Reprinted by permission of Farrar, Straus and Giroux, LLC.

Editor's Note: sourced from a press release posted on "The Official Website of the Government of Antigua and Barbuda."

"What Is an African American Classic?": by Henry Louis Gates Jr. copyright © 2008 by Henry Louis Gates, Jr., General Introduction from *Twelve Years a Slave*, by Solomon Northup. Used by permission of Penguin Books, an imprint of Penguin Publishing Group, a division of Penguin Random House LLC.

"New Black Scribe": from "Introduction," copyright © 1990 by Terry McMillan, from *Breaking Ice: An Anthology of Contemporary African-American Fiction*, edited by Terry McMillan. Used by permission of Viking Books, an imprint of Penguin Publishing Group, a division of Penguin Random House LLC; and by permission of The Friedrich Agency. Accessed from a reprint in *The African American Book of Values*, edited by Steven Barboza (Doubleday, 1998).

"MFA vs. POC," copyright © 2014 by Junot Díaz. First published in *Dismantle: An Anthology of Writing from the VONA / Voices Writing Workshop* (Thread Makes Blanket Press; 2014). Accessed from the Page-Turner blog of *The New Yorker*, April 30, 2014. Reprinted by permission of Aragi, Inc., literary agency, New York, NY. For more information about VONA, visit vonacommunity.org /community/index.php.

"Create Dangerously": from *Create Dangerously*, by Edwidge Danticat, Princeton University Press. Copyright © 2010 by Edwidge Danticat. Reprinted by permission of Princeton University Press.

"How to Write": by Colson Whitehead. A version of this op-ed appeared in print on July 29, 2012, on page BR8 of the *New York Times Book Review* with the

BONUS FEATURE

ACKNOWLEDGMENTS

*Gratitude to all whose soaring spirits
are included in this anthology.
To all who read it—you!
And we thank "the village"...*

For making it happen:
- Victoria Sanders & Associates: Victoria Sanders, Bernadette Baker, Deborah Jayne
- 37 Ink | Atria Books | Simon & Schuster: Judith Curr, Dawn Davis, Yona Deshommes, Lindsay Newton, Mark LaFlaur, Lourdes Lopez, Patricia Callahan, Kristen Strange, and Lisa Nicholas
- Deirdre Smerillo of Smerillo Associates
- All the publishers, agents, and administrators who granted rights and permissions

For sending me the Foreword before even saying yes:
- My favorite poet and cherished friend, Nikki Giovanni
- Thanks to Virginia Fowler, too.

For the resources and research:
- Anguilla Library Services: Jansie Webster, Anthea Roach
- Seattle Public Library: Douglass-Truth Branch, Central Main Library

For the encouraging word:
Shelia Baynes
Amy Berkower & Dan Weiss
Rene Boatman of Toni Morrison's office
Dan & Blythe Brown
Carolyn Denard
Audrey Edwards
dream hampton
Winona Hauge
Sherille & Franklin Hughes
Melinda Goddard & Terry Brady
Chris Jackson
Benilde Little
Susan Long-Walsh
Rick Simonson
Geraldine Smith
Marlene F. Watson
Erlene Berry Wilson

Anguilla Lit Fest Committee:
Candis Niles
Sherille Hughes
Carrolle Devonish
Jahia Semeria-Esposito
Kay Ferguson
Collette Jones-Chin
Ronya Foy-Connor
Carla Harris
Trudy Nixon
Reginald Oliver
Anthea Roach
Jansie Webster
Pam Webster

For crowdsourcing the choice of title on Facebook:
Marisol Alfaro, Adunni Anderson, Amena Oliver Anderson,
Andrea Anderson, Sue Annetts, Florence Anthony, Joyce
Altaras, Jennifer Atherley, Cerise Banks, Oluwakemi Linda
Banks, Shelia T. Baynes, Deborah Boomer, Sharon Breland,
Anique Oliver Brewer, John Phillip Burns, Alta Cannady, Janice
Carter, Veronica Chambers, Ahmondyllah Cole, Mikel Colson,
Copper Cunningham, Sarah Dean, Rachel Christmas Derrick,
Yona Deshommes, Suzan Williams Donahue, Yvonne Durant,
Janine Edwards, Aleta Felder, Lauren Francis-Sharma, the late
Arlene Bailey Franklin, Richard L. Gant, Melinda Goddard,
Mondella Jones, Joyce Harley, Aleeyah Oliver Hatcher, Audrey
Horn, Ziba Kashif, Linda Marie Kessler, Meko Lawson, Andrea
Lloyd, Susan Long-Walsh, Eugene Mackey, James A. Manning,
Sandra Martin, Claire McIntosh, Trudy Nixon, Reginald
Oliver, Renee Oliver, Bahia Oliver-Mays, Cathy Ranieri,
Bonnie Richardson-Lake, Teresa Ridley, Lorraine T. Rowe,
Victoria Sanders, Geoff Simmons, Sandra Sims, Henry Smith,
Tracey Brown Stephens, TaRessa Stovall, Anthony Thomas,
Linda Villarosa, Paula Ward, Leslie Williams, Carla Wills,
Charles Wilson, Andre S. Wooten, Verleeta Wooten, Phyllis
Yasutake

The family cheerleaders:
My husband, Reginald Oliver
Anique Oliver Brewer & Jonathan Brewer
Ahmondyllah & Shawn Cole
Aleeyah & Solomon Hatcher
Amena Oliver
Malcolm Oliver
Andre & Daphne Wooten
Vicki Stokes
Gloria Leonard

*To the memory of my late dad, Judge Charles M. Stokes,
reading his daily* Seattle Times, GQ, Time,
and researching in his law volumes

*In the beginning was the Word: The first words I heard
were those of my mother's voice, reading bedtime stories to
my brother, sister, and me. Loving gratitude to my mother,
Josephine Stokes, the grade-school teacher, librarian,
and reading specialist who instilled in her children and
grandchildren the love of books from womb to tomb.*

*For giving me hope in the next
generation of readers, my granddaughter:
Anzala Olivia Joy Brewer*

ABOUT THE EDITOR

Stephanie Stokes Oliver has enjoyed a career spent entirely in magazine and book publishing. Formerly fashion and beauty merchandising editor at *Glamour*, editor of *Essence* magazine, editor in chief of Essence.com, and founding editor in chief of *Heart & Soul*, she most recently served as vice president of Unity Publishing.

Working from Anguilla in the Caribbean and in her American hometown of Seattle, Oliver currently writes books, scouts literary projects, teaches college courses on publishing, coaches authors, and provides editorial services under her consultancy SSO Media. A founding member of the Anguilla Literary Foundation, she is the author curator for the annual Anguilla Lit Fest.

Achieving her greatest desire, to become an author, Oliver has published three previous books: *Daily Cornbread: 365 Secrets for a Healthy Mind, Body, and Spirit*; *Seven Soulful Secrets for Finding Your Purpose and Minding Your Mission*; and *Song for My Father: Memoir of an All-American Family*.